First Steps wit

About the Author

Carolyn Hughes first entered the world of computers when her family acquired a Sinclair ZX80. They have since added to their collection a ZX81, a ZX Spectrum and a BBC micro.

Because of her teaching background – she has taught in a variety of schools from Infant to Secondary – she is particularly interested in children's involvement with computers, both in education and just for fun. She has three children and runs a computer club at the Junior School her two boys attend.

As well as books she writes educational software for the ZX81 and ZX Spectrum.

CAROLYN HUGHES

First Steps with Your Spectrum

with illustrations by
BRYAN READING

An Armada Original

First Steps with Your Spectrum was first published
in the U.K. in 1983 in Armada by Fontana Paperbacks,
8 Grafton Street, London W1X 3LA

Printed and bound in Great Britain at
the University Press, Oxford.

Contents

1 What computers can do *(with your help).* 11

2 Getting started. *Plugging in. Tuning the T.V.* 14

3 The Spectrum speaks to you. *Using the keyboard.* PRINT *and* ENTER. 17

4 Mistakes. *What to do when the computer doesn't understand.* DELETE. 20

5 The Spectrum remembers. *Numbering your program lines.* RUN. *Blank lines.* 22

6 A New Program. *Clearing the computer.* NEW. *Capital letters.* 26

7 Strings. *Quote marks and characters.* 28

8 Cursors. K *and* L *cursors. Keywords.* 29

9 Spacers. *Comma, semi-colon, apostrophe.* 31

10 The Spectrum waits for your answer INPUT 34

11 Little Boxes. 36
String variables.

12 Another way into the boxes 38
When to use LET.

13 Numbers. 40
Add, subtract, multiply and divide. Priorities.

14 More boxes. 43
Number variables.

15 Making changes. 45
The program cursor. EDIT.
The arrows. LIST.

16 The Spectrum makes a decision. 48
IF . . . THEN. CLS. STOP. *The colon.*

17 The Spectrum does it again. 51
GO TO. *How to get out of a loop.*
BREAK.

18 The Spectrum chooses a number. 55
The E cursor. RND *and* INT.
Scroll?

19 Loops for counting. 61
Loop variables. FOR .. TO .. NEXT.
PAUSE

20 The Spectrum draws a picture. 65
Graphics characters and the G *cursor.*
PRINT AT. CONT*inue.*

21 Colours. 75
BORDER, PAPER, INK.

22 Moving shapes. 79
Making things move up, down and across the screen. STEP.

23 Beep, beep. 82
How to make music and sounds.

24 INKEY $. 85

25 Saving your programs on cassette. 87
How to SAVE, VERIFY *and* LOAD.

26 Planning your programs. 94
Writing down what you aim to do.
Variables. Using REM.

27 You could do it like this. 99
Suggestions for answering the
questions in the earlier chapters.

28 Games 106

Index 128

Preface

When I started running a computer club at my sons' Junior school, using the ZX81 and ZX Spectrum, I realised just how fascinated children are by computers, and how keen they are to start programming. However, the manuals and programming books which are available were written for adults. This book aims to fill the need for a guide which will take the young reader gently through the rudiments of Spectrum BASIC.

Introduction

There are lots of books written about the Spectrum. They were not written with *you* in mind. This book was.

Although you may never get to fly a space shuttle to the moon, or fight a dragon in a dark underground cave system, the Spectrum can let you experience these things.

To imitate a space shuttle flight, or to create a fantasy world where you can defeat evil wizards and witches, and find fabulous treasure, you need to be able to write a *program* for the computer.

Programming a computer like the Spectrum is exciting, and surprisingly easy. Carolyn Hughes has helped many people learn to program the Spectrum, and in this book she's chosen an easy-to-understand approach to the subject.

You probably won't need anybody's help to master the Spectrum, now that you have this book. Just spend a few hours with it, with your computer turned on, and you'll soon be making the computer obey your every command. What's more, as you learn about the Spectrum, you'll realise you're learning a lot about computers in general. You'll soon know much, much more than do most of the grown-ups you see around you. And that's well worth it for its own sake.

It's time to start discovering how much fun it can be to get a computer to follow your every wish.

Tim Hartnell,
London, March 1983

Tim Hartnell is founding editor of *ZX Computing* magazine, and author of a number of popular computer books.

CHAPTER 1

What computers can do

Welcome to the band of Spectrum users! I expect you are now wondering just how much this little black box can do. Well, there are a great many things computers can do, but only with our help.

Although the Spectrum may look small, it has a large memory, and can work things out extremely fast. If you give it details of the pupils in a school, for example, it can in a few seconds give you the answers to questions such as which boys aged under ten live in a particular street – a job which would be very slow and boring if you had to do it yourself.

It can also help you to learn. Say you had to learn the names and positions of the rivers in Australia. The Spectrum could show you them on the screen, ask you to name each one, and correct you on the ones you got wrong.

Computers can do jobs in factories too. Many cars are made by robots, linked to computers, which work fast and accurately and don't need tea breaks. At the moment, the computers that do this sort of work are larger and more expensive than the Spectrum, but you may find your Spectrum can be made to do a similar type of job, such as controlling a model railway.

It sounds as though we humans aren't needed any more, doesn't it? We are, though, because computers will only do what they are told to do, and they can do nothing unless human beings show them how.

When your Spectrum was being made, it was taught how to do mathematical calculations (addition, subtraction, multiplication, division and also other more complicated ones).

It was also taught to understand a language called BASIC. If you want your Spectrum to work for you, you will have to learn to use BASIC, and it is the aim of this book to get you started. BASIC is very like English, so you won't find it difficult.

CHAPTER 2

Getting Started

Put your Spectrum on a table near to a television set. If you have a colour T.V. then you will be able to see your programs in colour. If you only have a black and white set, don't worry, your Spectrum will still work, but in shades of grey. The only T.V. sets which are no good are very old ones which cannot get BBC 2.

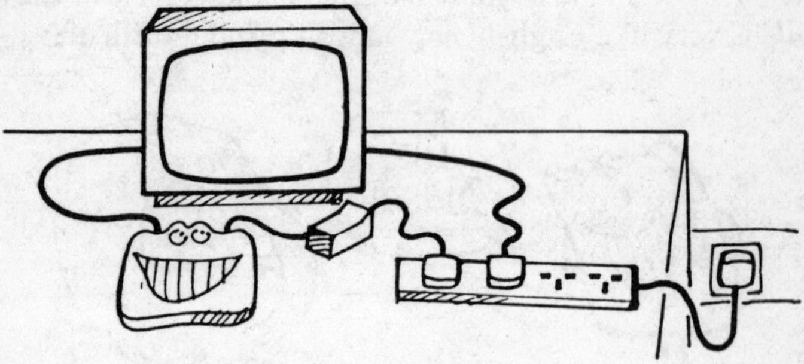

The Spectrum will need to be plugged in to the electricity. If you only have one electric socket you will need an adaptor, so that the television and the computer can share the electricity.

Later on you will need to use a cassette recorder too, so it would be worthwhile getting an adaptor which can take three or more plugs.

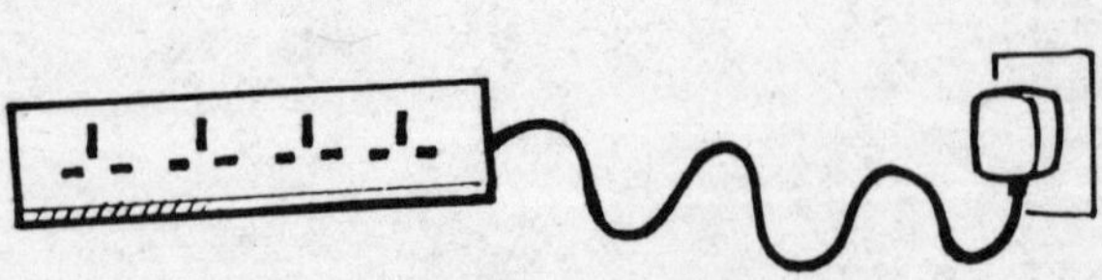

With your Spectrum is a lead which looks like this:

The pointed end goes into the Spectrum's T.V. socket.

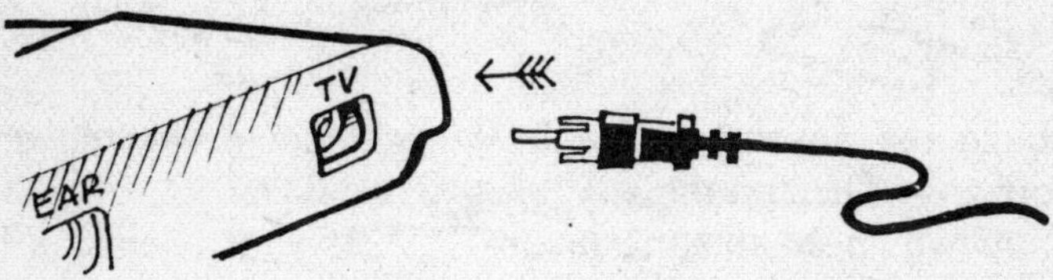

The other end goes into the aerial socket of the T.V. If your television has two aerial sockets, use the one marked U.H.F.

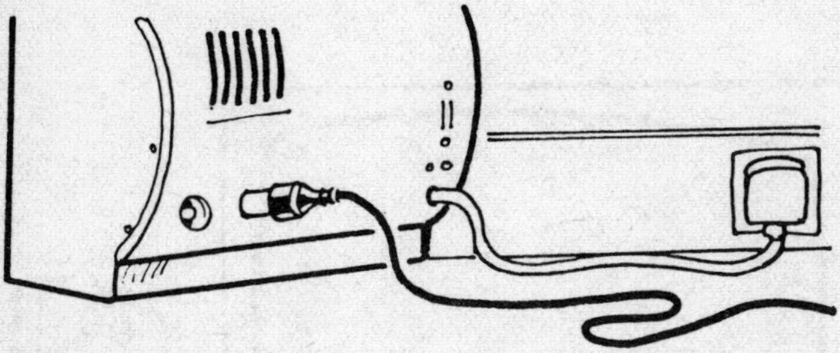

Now you need the black power box.

One end plugs into the electricity, the other into the Spectrum.

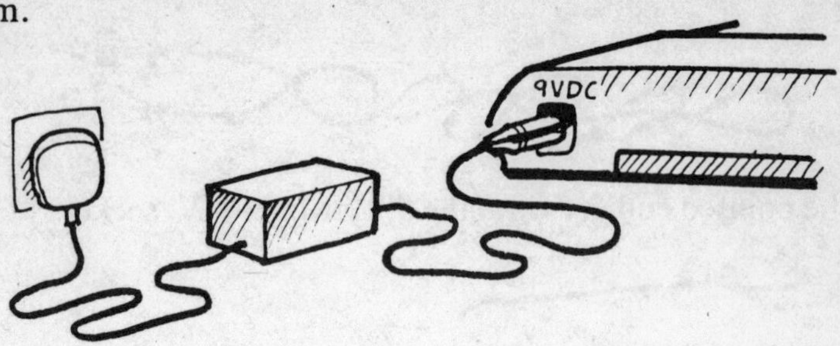

Turn the volume of the T.V. right down. Switch on the electricity. Turn on the T.V.

You will need to tune in the T.V. If your television has a button for each channel, choose a spare one that you do not use for watching BBC or ITV.

Now turn the tuning knob until the screen looks like this:

Your Spectrum is ready to work for you.

CHAPTER 3

The Spectrum speaks to you

The Spectrum uses the TV screen to speak to you. You have to tell it what to say, though!

We are going to make the Spectrum say hello to you. You will need to type in

PRINT "hello"

Turn over to find out just how to do this.

1. Press the key with PRINT on it.
2. Put your finger on the SYMBOL SHIFT key and hold it down.
3. Press the key with the quote marks " on it. (It's the same key as PRINT).
4. Take your finger off SYMBOL SHIFT.
5. Type the letters of hello.
6. Put your finger on SYMBOL SHIFT and press " again.

Your T.V. screen should look like this:

Now press ENTER. It's just below PRINT.

The Spectrum has obeyed your command and printed hello. The OK message at the bottom of the screen is the Spectrum's way of telling you that it has done what you asked.

Press ENTER again and the screen is clear except for the flashing K at the bottom.

CHAPTER 4

Mistakes

If you don't speak the computer's language correctly it won't understand you.

Try typing in

PRINT "hello

Press ENTER and see what happens. You get a flashing question mark because the Spectrum did not understand. Put in the " and press ENTER. All should now be well.

What do you do if you make a typing or a spelling mistake?

Above the top right key is the word DELETE. This is the key we use to rub things out.

Type in

PRINT "helo"

You've missed out an l!

Now, put your finger on CAPS SHIFT and keep it down. Press the DELETE key and the flashing L will eat up the letter to its left. Keep your fingers down and another letter will disappear. Be careful. If you hold the DELETE key down too long all your typing will be gone!

Now you can type your command in again without any mistakes.

CHAPTER 5

The Spectrum remembers

Now the Spectrum is obeying your commands, but it would be much easier for you if it remembered your instructions. Then you could get it to do the same things again without all that typing in again.

It will remember, if you put your command into a program.

A program is simply a list of instructions, with a number by each one so that the computer knows which order to do them in.

We usually number the program lines in steps of ten, instead of steps of one, so that if we find we have left something out we can fit it in.

Type in

10 PRINT "apples"

Press ENTER.
Line 10 will move up to the top of the screen.
It is now in the Spectrum's memory.

Type in

20 PRINT "bananas" (Press ENTER)
30 PRINT "pears" (Press ENTER)

If you discover after you have pressed ENTER that the line of the program is not quite as you want it, just type the line again, and press ENTER. The Spectrum will put your new line in place of the old one.

When you are ready for the computer to obey your instructions, press RUN and then ENTER.

You should have a neat list of fruits on the screen, and the OK message at the bottom. The number 30 after OK means the Spectrum finished your instructions at line 30.

Press ENTER. Now you can see the listing of your program again.

Type in

25 PRINT "grapes" (Press ENTER)

Line 30 has moved down to make room for line 25.
The Spectrum knows its numbers!

RUN the program again. Don't forget to press ENTER after RUN.

Type in three more lines:

```
15 PRINT
22 PRINT
27 PRINT
```

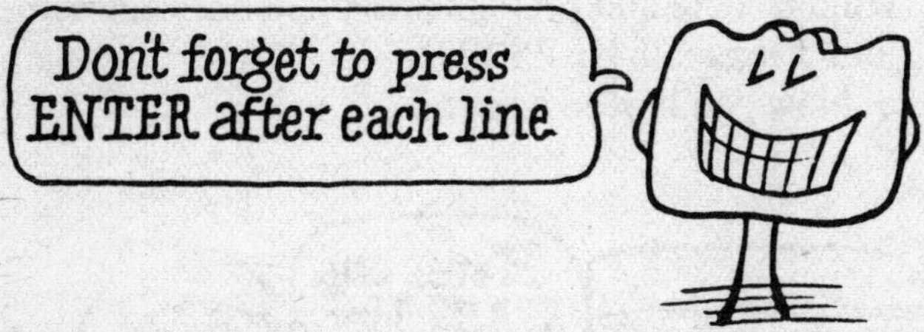

RUN the program and see what these lines did.

CHAPTER 6

A New Program

Are you ready to write a new program now? Tell the computer by pressing NEW. It's on the same key as the letter A. Now press ENTER.

The Spectrum's memory is now clear again for your next program.

Let's get the computer to print your name.

Type in

```
10 PRINT "
```

Now you'll need a capital letter. Put your finger on CAPS SHIFT. Hold it there and press the first letter of your name.

Take your finger off CAPS SHIFT and finish typing your first name. Now you'll need a space.

Type in your surname, with a capital letter. Put in the quote marks and press ENTER.

RUN the program and then press ENTER to see your program listing again.

For you to do

Add some more lines to the program so that the computer will print your address as well. Look for the comma and the full stop on the keys. They are in red, so when you need them you will have to hold down SYMBOL SHIFT as you type them.

If you get stuck, turn to Chapter 27, page 99.

CHAPTER 7

Strings

All our programs so far have had strings in them.

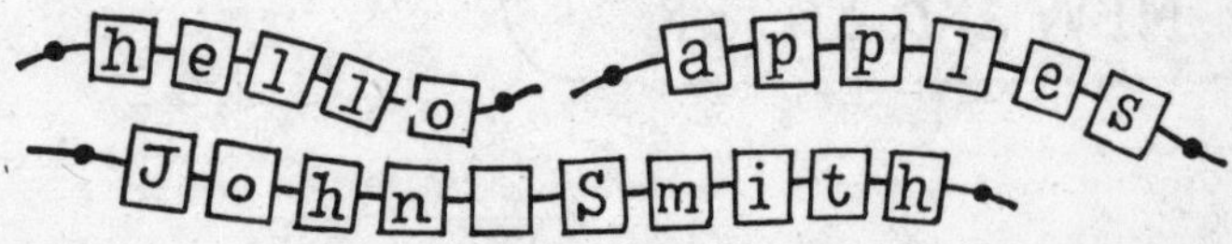

A string is just a set of letters, or numbers, or other symbols, such as + or *. We call these 'characters'. C, £ and + are all characters.

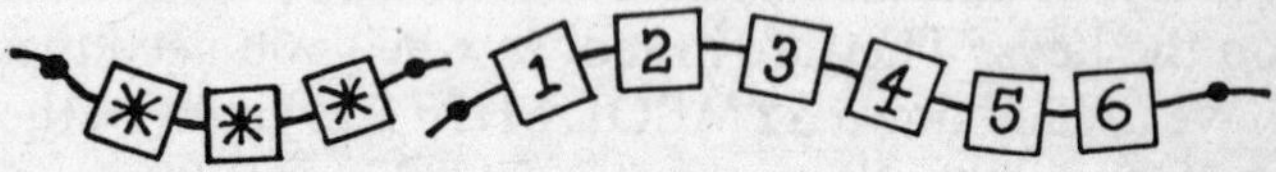

When you want a string to be printed on the screen, just put quote marks " at the beginning and the end, and the computer will print everything inside the quote marks. You can think of the quote marks as knots in the ends of the string, to stop any of the letters getting lost.

You can have an empty string, with nothing, not even a space, between the quote marks. It is sometimes called a null string.

CHAPTER 8

Cursors

I expect you have been wondering about the flashing K and L that often appear on the screen. They are called cursors, and show that the Spectrum is ready and waiting for you to type something in.

The second, third and bottom rows of keys have words on them, as well as letters of the alphabet. These are called keywords. If you press one of these keys when the cursor is K, the key word will appear on the screen. You've already used the keywords PRINT and RUN.

If you press an alphabet key when the cursor is L, you will get the letter on the screen.

The top row of keys, which are numbers, will print you a number whether the cursor is K or L.

Try pressing a few keys. Watch the cursor change from K to L. When you've finished, rub out what you've printed using the DELETE key. (Look back at chapter 4 for this if you need to).

As well as keywords, letters and numbers, the keys have words and symbols on them in red. To make these appear on the screen you hold down SYMBOL SHIFT and press the key you want.

For you to do

Write a program to print a line of stars along the top of the screen.

CHAPTER 9

Spacers

Spacers help you to put things where you want them on the screen.

Type in this program and RUN it.

```
1Ø PRINT "wheel"
2Ø PRINT "barrow"
```

Now change line 1Ø by typing

```
1Ø PRINT "wheel",
```

RUN the program again.

The comma tells the Spectrum to move to the other half of the screen and then print the next item.

Change line 1Ø again. Type

```
1Ø PRINT "wheel";
```

You will find the semi-colon ; on the same key as the letter O. You will need SYMBOL SHIFT as it is in red.

When you RUN the program again you will get

The semi-colon tells the computer that it must not leave any spaces before it prints the next item.

If you want to use , or ; as spacers they must go *outside* the quote marks. If you put them inside they will be part of the string, and will be printed on the screen as the comma was in your address.

Now press NEW and ENTER ready for the next program.

This spacer, which looks like an apostrophe, is useful if you have a long sentence to type in. Type in

```
10 PRINT ''The day after tomorrow will be Wednesday''
```

Now RUN this short program.

You need ′

Type this line in very carefully:

10 PRINT "The day after tomorrow will be" ′ "Wednesday"

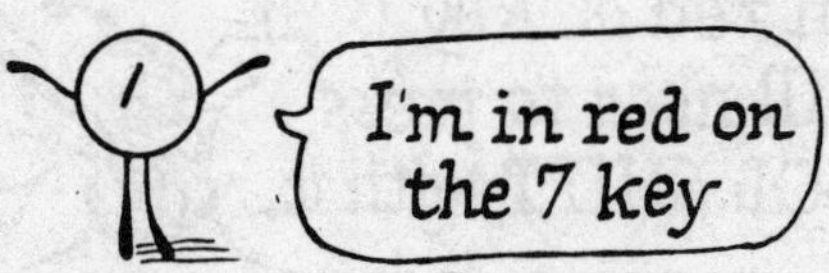

′ tells the Spectrum to move to the next line.

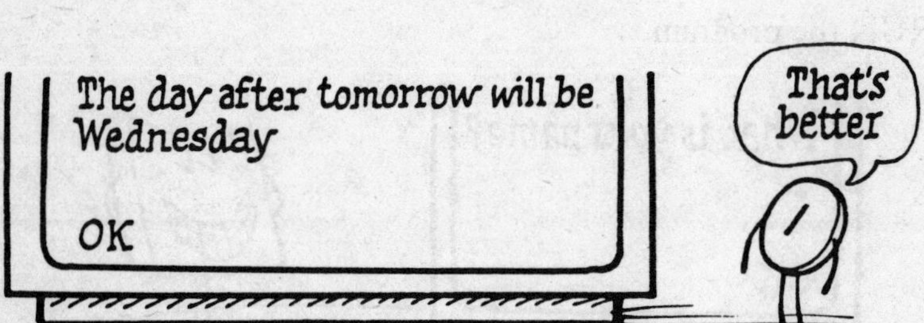

CHAPTER 10

The Spectrum waits for your answer

Now you know how to make the Spectrum say what you want it to. You could get it to ask you a question.

Clear the computer by pressing NEW and then ENTER. Now type in this program.

10 PRINT "What is your name?"

RUN the program.

The Spectrum didn't wait for your answer, did it!

Add these two lines to the program.

```
2Ø INPUT a $
3Ø PRINT "Hello   "; a$
```

RUN the program again.
When you see the flashing "L" type in your name and press ENTER.

This time the Spectrum not only waited for your answer, it remembered your name and addressed you by it.

For you to do:-

Alter the program so that the Spectrum leaves one blank line between asking your name and saying "Hello". You may be able to find more than one way of doing it.

CHAPTER 11

Little Boxes

This is how the Spectrum remembered your name:

In its memory it has a part specially for storing strings. This section of the memory is like 26 little boxes, which start off empty, with blank labels on them.

At line 2Ø of the last program the Spectrum saw INPUT a$. It didn't think, "Good, I've got some dollars coming to me!" It knew there was a string coming and it had to get a box ready for it.

First of all it looked to see if any of the labels had a$ on them already. They hadn't, so it gave the name a$ to one of the boxes and waited to see what you were going to put in it.

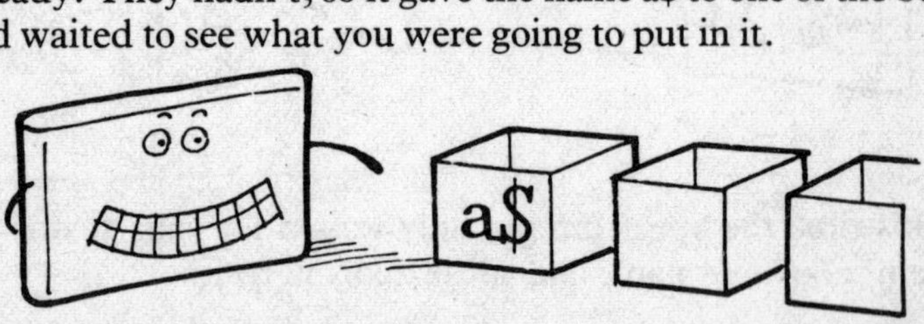

You typed in your name, which then went into the box with the label a$.

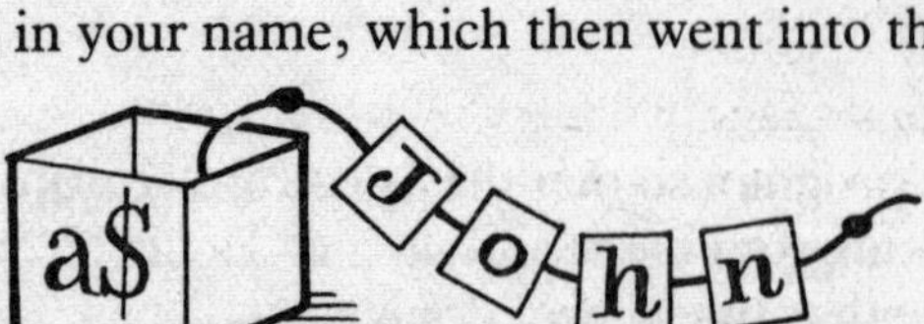

At line 3Ø, after printing "Hello", the computer looked in the box a$ and printed the string it saw in there.

Your name is still in the box a$. It will stay there until you put something else in instead, or until you press RUN, which will empty all the boxes.

Check that your name is still there by typing PRINT a$ and then pressing ENTER.

RUN the program again, but this time when you are asked, "What is your name?" type in a different name. The new name is now in the box a$.

a$ is called a string variable, because you can vary, or change, the string which it holds.

You can have up to 26 string variables in a program. (Remember the 26 little boxes?). They can be called a$, b$, and so on, up to z$.

For you to do

Write a program in which the Spectrum asks you the name of the town or village where you live. You type it in, and the computer stores it in box p$. The computer prints the name of your town. Then it says this is a pleasant place to live. Make sure the words are set out well on the screen.

CHAPTER 12

Another way into the boxes

You can tell the Spectrum what to put in a string variable box before you RUN the program. You do it like this:

```
10 LET a$ = "computer"
```

As soon as you RUN this program the Spectrum will label a box a$ and put the word "computer" in it.

This would be useful in a long program if you wanted the word "computer" printed several times. Instead of having to type PRINT "computer" every time you would just type PRINT a$, which is much quicker.

Mind you don't ask the Spectrum to print the contents of a box before you've put anything in it. It's not a magician.

CHAPTER 13

Numbers

Now we come to something the Spectrum knows a lot about already.

Let's test its Maths. Type
PRINT 132 + 499 (Press ENTER)
It's certainly quick at addition.
Now try a subtraction question:
PRINT 2954 – 877

The signs for multiplication and division are different from the usual ones.

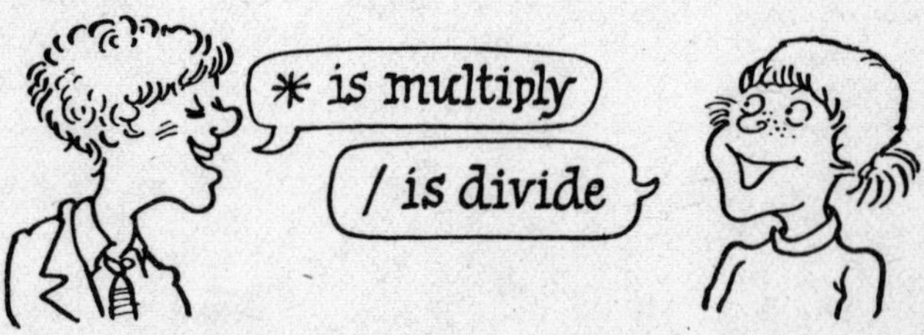

Find them on the key-board. They are in red, on the bottom row. Give the Spectrum some * and / questions. It can manage very large numbers, but if the numbers are too large it will give the answer in a way you probably won't understand.

If you ask it to do a question with a mixture of + − * and / in it, the Spectrum has a special order of working them out.

Ask it to PRINT 2 + 3 * 4

Did it give the answer you expected, or did you expect it to say 2Ø?

When it has a mixed question, the Spectrum does multiplication and division first, and then addition and subtraction.

If you want it to do the addition or subtraction first, you must put that part inside brackets.

Try PRINT (2 + 3) * 4

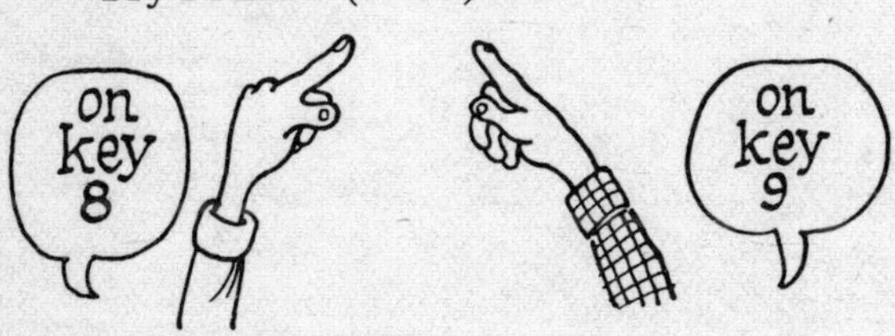

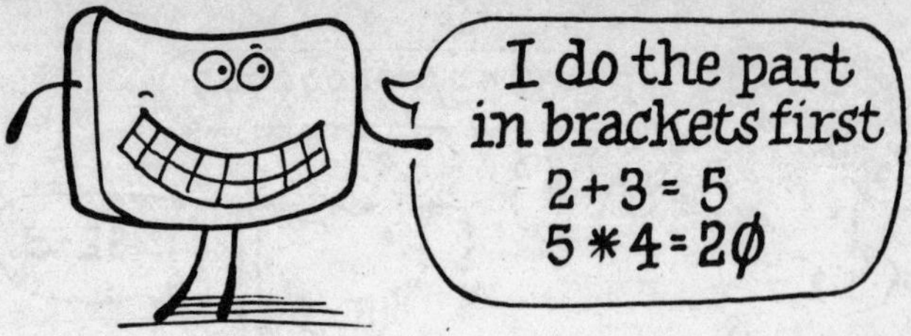

For you to do

1. Try some questions of your own and see if you get the answers you expect.
2. Find out the difference between

   PRINT 5 – 3
   and
   PRINT "5 – 3"

CHAPTER 14

More boxes

In Chapter 1Ø you put a string into a box called a$. Numbers, too, can be stored in boxes.

Type in this program

```
1Ø INPUT a
2Ø INPUT b
3Ø LET c = a + b
4Ø PRINT c
```

When you RUN it, all you will see on the screen is a flashing L. This tells you the Spectrum is waiting for a number, so type one in and press ENTER. The computer will put this number in box a (line 1Ø). The L is still flashing so enter another number. This goes in box b (line 2Ø). The computer adds together your two numbers and puts the answer into box c (line 3Ø). Then it prints the contents of box c (line 4Ø).

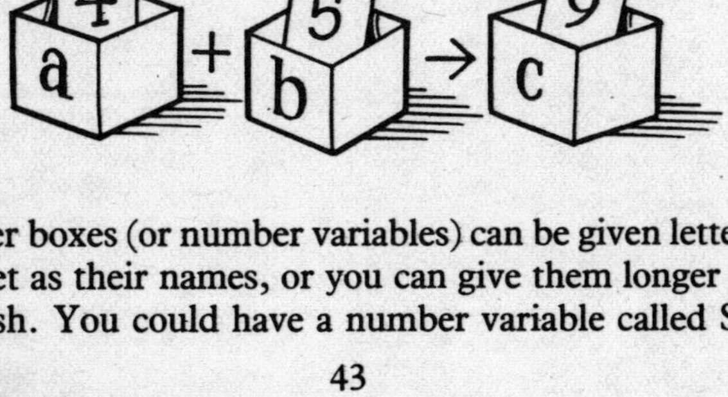

Number boxes (or number variables) can be given letters of the alphabet as their names, or you can give them longer names if you wish. You could have a number variable called Score, or

ANSWER 5. This can sometimes be useful as it helps you remember what the number in the box does.

For you to do

Write a program where you put in two numbers (call them NUMBER 1 and NUMBER 2) and the computer multiplies them, putting the answer into ANSWER. Don't forget to tell the computer to PRINT ANSWER at the end.

CHAPTER 15

Making changes

So far we have met two ways of changing what you have typed in. If you have not yet pressed ENTER, you can use the delete key to rub things out. If you have already pressed ENTER, you can change a program line by typing it again.

You may have noticed > after a line number in your program. It is called the program cursor and points to the line you have just entered.

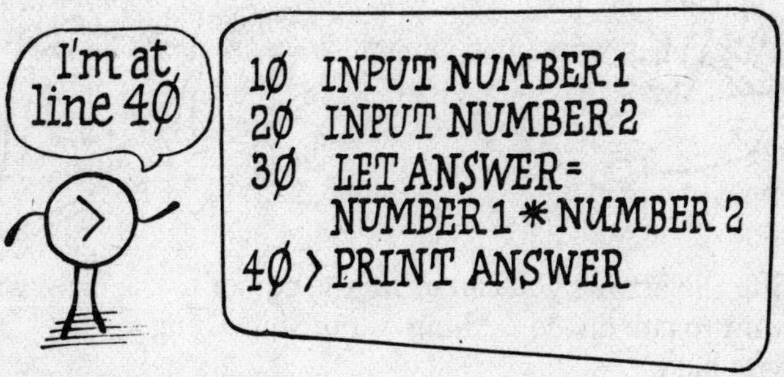

Hold your finger down on CAPS SHIFT and press the key with EDIT above it.

The Spectrum will copy the line and it will appear at the bottom of the screen, with the cursor flashing after the line number.

Above keys 5, 6, 7 and 8 you will see four arrows:

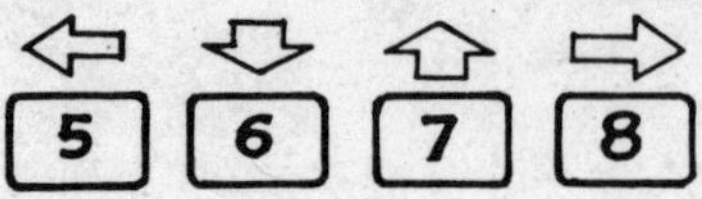

Put your finger on CAPS SHIFT and press 8

The cursor will move to the right. If you hold your finger down on 8 the cursor will move right to the end of the line.

Now press CAPS SHIFT and 5, and the cursor will move left again.

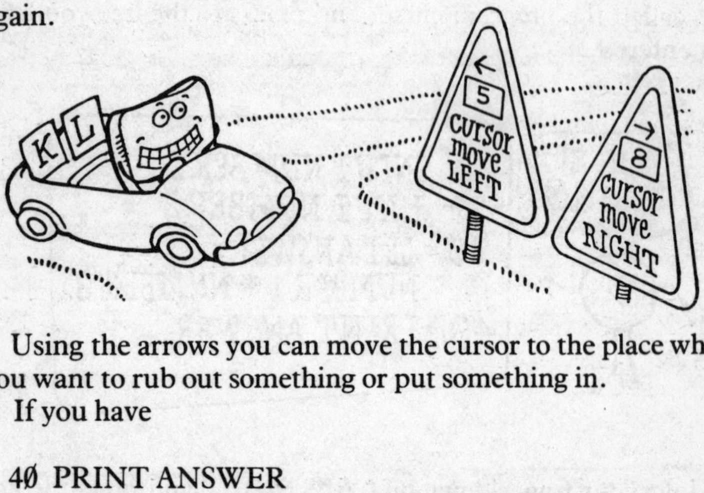

Using the arrows you can move the cursor to the place where you want to rub out something or put something in.

If you have

4Ø PRINT ANSWER

at the bottom of the screen, move the cursor so that it is between PRINT and ANSWER. Now type in

"The answer is ";

Press ENTER and your new, longer line 4Ø is in the program.

What do you do if you need to change line 1Ø?

Put your finger on CAPS SHIFT and press 7. The program cursor will move up to the line above. If you want the program cursor to move down, press CAPS SHIFT and 6

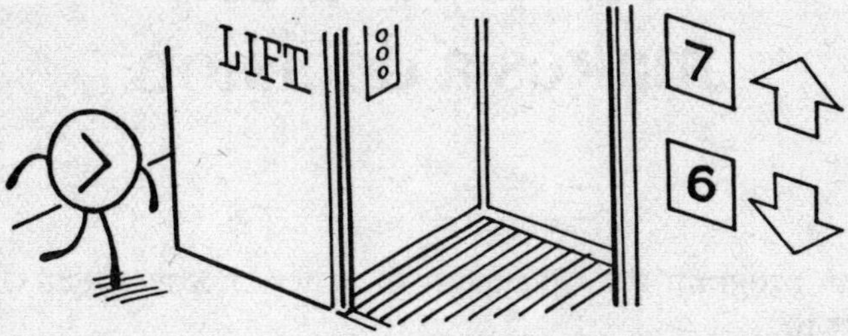

When the program cursor is at the correct line, press CAPS SHIFT and EDIT and down it comes to the bottom of the screen.

Practice using the four arrows, and EDIT. When you want the line at the bottom of the screen to go back into the program, just press ENTER.

A quick way of moving the program cursor to the line you want is to use LIST, which is the keyword on key K. Press LIST and then ENTER and the program cursor will move to the first line of the program. LIST 2Ø will take it to line 2Ø, LIST 3Ø to line 3Ø and so on.

CHAPTER 16

The Spectrum makes a decision

In this program the Spectrum is rather choosy about who it speaks to.

```
10 PRINT "What is your name?"
20 INPUT a$
30 CLS
40 IF a$ < > "Mickey Mouse" THEN
PRINT "I don't speak to people called" ' a$
```

< > means ' is not equal to '

RUN the program
What does CLS do?

At line 4Ø the Spectrum looked into a$. If it did not find Mickey Mouse it gave a rude answer.

If it *did* find Mickey Mouse it didn't print anything. Let's change this.

Bring line 4Ø down to the bottom of the screen, using EDIT. (Look back at the last chapter if necessary). Move the cursor right to the end of the line and put in : STOP

Press ENTER to put the new line 40 into the program.

Now type in

5Ø PRINT "Pleased to meet you."

RUN the program. Give your name as Mickey Mouse and see what happens.

Because Mickey Mouse *was* in a$ the Spectrum skipped over line 4Ø and went straight to line 5Ø.

Up to now we had only given the computer one instruction in each line. Line 4Ø now has two.

There must be a colon : between each instruction.

For you to do:

1. Find out what happens if you don't have : STOP in line 4Ø. Edit line 4Ø and delete : STOP. Then RUN the program and give your own name.

2. The Spectrum's favourite food is chips. Write a program in which:-

1Ø The computer asks you what your favourite food is.
2Ø You type in your answer, which goes into f$.
3Ø The screen clears.
4Ø If you did not answer "chips" the Spectrum tells you it does not like your food, it prefers chips.
5Ø If you answered "chips" the Spectrum says it agrees with you.

CHAPTER 17

The Spectrum does it again

Type in this short program:

```
1Ø INPUT a
2Ø PRINT a
3Ø GO TO 1Ø
```

RUN it. When you see the flashing L, type in a number. The Spectrum prints it and then waits for another. How do you get it to stop?

Instead of entering a number, press SYMBOL SHIFT and STOP, then ENTER.

Now try:

```
10 INPUT a$
20 PRINT a$
30 GO TO 10
```

The flashing "L" tells you the computer is expecting a string. Just pressing SYMBOL SHIFT and STOP doesn't work this time. The Spectrum sees STOP as a string and put it into a$.

This is how to get round it. Delete the first set of quote marks, so you have L" in the corner of the screen. Now press SYMBOL SHIFT and STOP. You are out of the loop.

When you are writing programs you may accidentally get into a type of loop where STOP will not help. Here is an example:

```
10 LET n = 1
20 GO TO 10
```

When you RUN this program, all you see is a blank screen, with no cursor.

You need to break out of the loop.

The SPACE key also has the word BREAK on it. Put your finger on CAPS SHIFT and press BREAK SPACE

Press ENTER and you will see the listing of the program again.

Loops can be very useful, if you make sure the program tells the computer when to leave the loop. Here is an example:

```
10 PRINT "Give me a number."
20 INPUT n
30 IF n = 0 THEN STOP
40 CLS
50 PRINT n ; " * 12 = " ; n * 12
60 GO TO 10
```

When you want to stop the program running you just enter the number 0.

For you to do

Write a program where:

1Ø The computer asks for a name.
2Ø You type one in. It goes into n$
3Ø If you typed "end" the computer stops.
4Ø The computer prints the name.
5Ø The computer goes back to the beginning of the program.

CHAPTER 18

The Spectrum chooses a number

In many games it is necessary for the computer to choose a number, without you knowing what it is. The Spectrum has in its memory a long list of numbers. It will choose one, at random, when you use RND.

RND is written in green above key T. To get it onto the screen we need the help of another cursor, the E cursor.

After clearing the computer with NEW, press both CAPS SHIFT and SYMBOL SHIFT at the same time and then lift your fingers off the keys.

The cursor should now be a flashing E. Now press the key with RND in green above it.

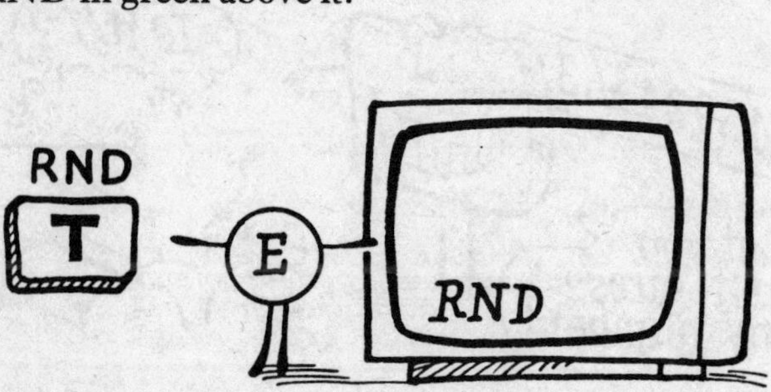

Delete RND and type in this program:

```
10 PRINT RND
20 GO TO 10
```

Always use the E cursor for RND. Do not type the letters one by one, or the computer will think it is a number variable, and go and look for a box called RND.

When you RUN the program the Spectrum prints a list of numbers and then asks you, "scroll?", meaning, "do you want me to move these numbers up the screen and print some more?" If you don't want any more, press N or SPACE. If you do, press any one of the other keys.

Look at the numbers on the screen. They're not the sort of numbers we'd want for a game, are they? It would be impossible to guess one of them.

We need bigger numbers, without all those decimals. Change the program to

```
10 PRINT INT (RND * 10) + 1
20 GO TO 10
```

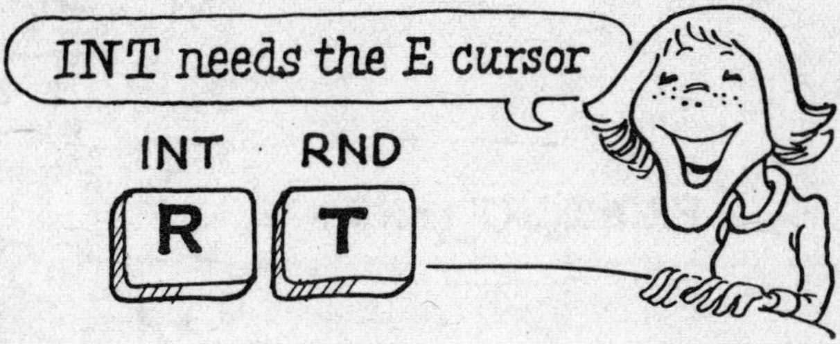

Run the program. Let the computer scroll the screen a few times, and you will see that the numbers it has chosen are all between 1 and 10.

In line 10, RND * 10 made the number bigger, INT cut off the digits after the decimal point, and +1 just made sure the computer never gave you the number 0.

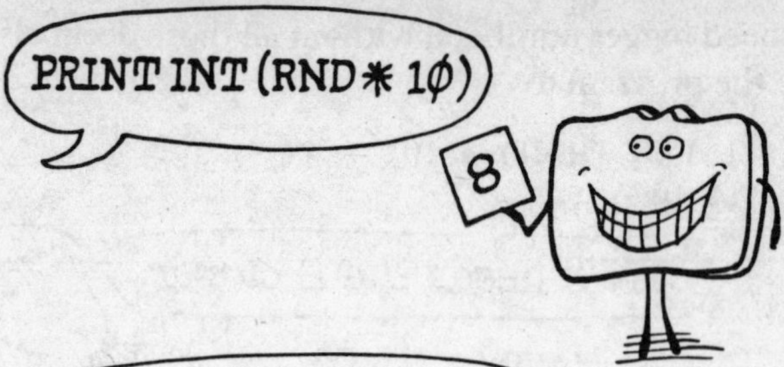

Do you know why we need brackets round RND * 1Ø? It is so that the computer does this part first.

Now we are ready for a guessing game.

```
1Ø LET a = INT (RND * 5) +1
2Ø PRINT "Guess my number."
3Ø PRINT "It is 1, 2, 3, 4 or 5."
4Ø INPUT b
5Ø PRINT b
6Ø IF b = a THEN PRINT "Right. You won." : STOP
7Ø PRINT "Wrong"
8Ø PRINT "Try again." : GO TO 4Ø
```

The Spectrum can never win this game. You get as many guesses as you need. Let's make it fairer. This time you will have only 3 chances.

We are going to use box g to store the number of guesses you have had. At the beginning you have had no guesses, so type in:

```
5 LET g = Ø
```

You put in your guess at line 4Ø (INPUT b), so after each guess we must add 1 to the number in g:

```
45 LET g = g + 1
```

When you have had 3 guesses you don't get any more tries, so we will need to change line 8Ø:

```
8Ø IF g < 3 THEN PRINT "Try again." GO TO 4Ø
```

< means "is less than."

Let the Spectrum congratulate itself if it wins:

```
9Ø PRINT "I won! It was "; a
```

For you to do

Write a program where:

1Ø The Spectrum chooses a number between 1 and 1ØØ, and puts it into a.
2Ø The Spectrum chooses a number between 1 and 1ØØ, and puts it into b
3Ø It adds a to b and puts the answer into c
4Ø It prints a ; " + " ; b ; " = " ;
5Ø You put in your try at the answer, which goes into box d.
6Ø The Spectrum prints your answer
7Ø If your answer is correct the Spectrum congratulates you. The program stops.
8Ø The Spectrum tells you the correct answer.

CHAPTER 19

Loops for counting

In the last chapter we gave one of the number variable boxes the label g and used it to count the number of guesses you'd had.

The Spectrum has, in fact, a special set of boxes, called loop variables, which are used just for counting. When you want to use one you give it a name. This must be a letter of the alphabet. Here is a program which will print the word "Spectrum" twenty times.

```
1Ø FOR L = 1 TO 2Ø
2Ø PRINT L, "Spectrum"
3Ø NEXT L
```

The Spectrum starts by labelling one of the loop variable boxes L and putting 1 into it.

Then it goes into the loop:

RUN the program and you will see the computer counting from 1 to 2Ø as it prints its name. You can make it count more slowly by telling it to PAUSE.

Put in

```
25 PAUSE 5Ø
```

The bigger the number after the word PAUSE, the longer the pause will be.

Here is a program to print the 9 times table up to 12 × 9:

```
1Ø FOR a = 1 TO 12
2Ø PRINT a;" *9= ";a*9
3Ø NEXT a
```

The computer will go round the loop 12 times. Each time, when it comes to line 2Ø, it will look into the box a and print the number it finds. Then it will print the string " * 9 = ". After that it will work out what a * 9 is and print the answer. NEXT a adds one to the number in a and sends the computer back to line 1Ø again.

Two programs for you to write

1. Tell the computer to print the 16 times table up to 20 times 16.
2. Tell it to print 704 question marks, without leaving any spaces between them.

CHAPTER 20

The Spectrum draws a picture

Along the top row of the keyboard, on the keys 1 to 8, you will see the graphics characters.

You can use these to make simple pictures. There is a graphics cursor, a flashing G, for printing these characters.

To get it into the screen, hold your finger on CAPS SHIFT and press key 9, which has the word GRAPHICS above it.
Now press the keys 1 to 8.

Put your finger on CAPS SHIFT and hold it down while you press the keys again.

These graphics characters are the opposite of the ones you got without CAPS SHIFT. The spaces are now black and the black parts are spaces.

When you have finished with the graphics characters, press 9 and you will have the L cursor back again.

Delete the shapes on the screen ready for this short program, which will draw a car.

1Ø PRINT "  "
2Ø PRINT "  "

When you have typed 1Ø PRINT " change the cursor to G by pressing CAPS SHIFT and 9.

The characters you need are 

Put your finger on CAPS SHIFT and press 2, 1, 3. Take your finger off CAPS SHIFT and press 9 to get the L cursor back. Now you can put in ".

Line 2Ø prints the wheels, two capital Os with a space in between.

Now write some programs of your own to draw pictures. You might try a factory, a horse, or an alien from outer space. It helps to draw them on squared paper before you start to write the program.

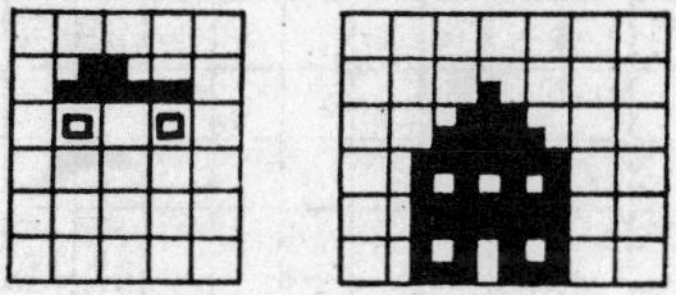

You might not always want your pictures in the top left corner of the screen.

Luckily there is a way to tell the Spectrum where to print on the screen.

Imagine your television screen is ruled into squares like this:

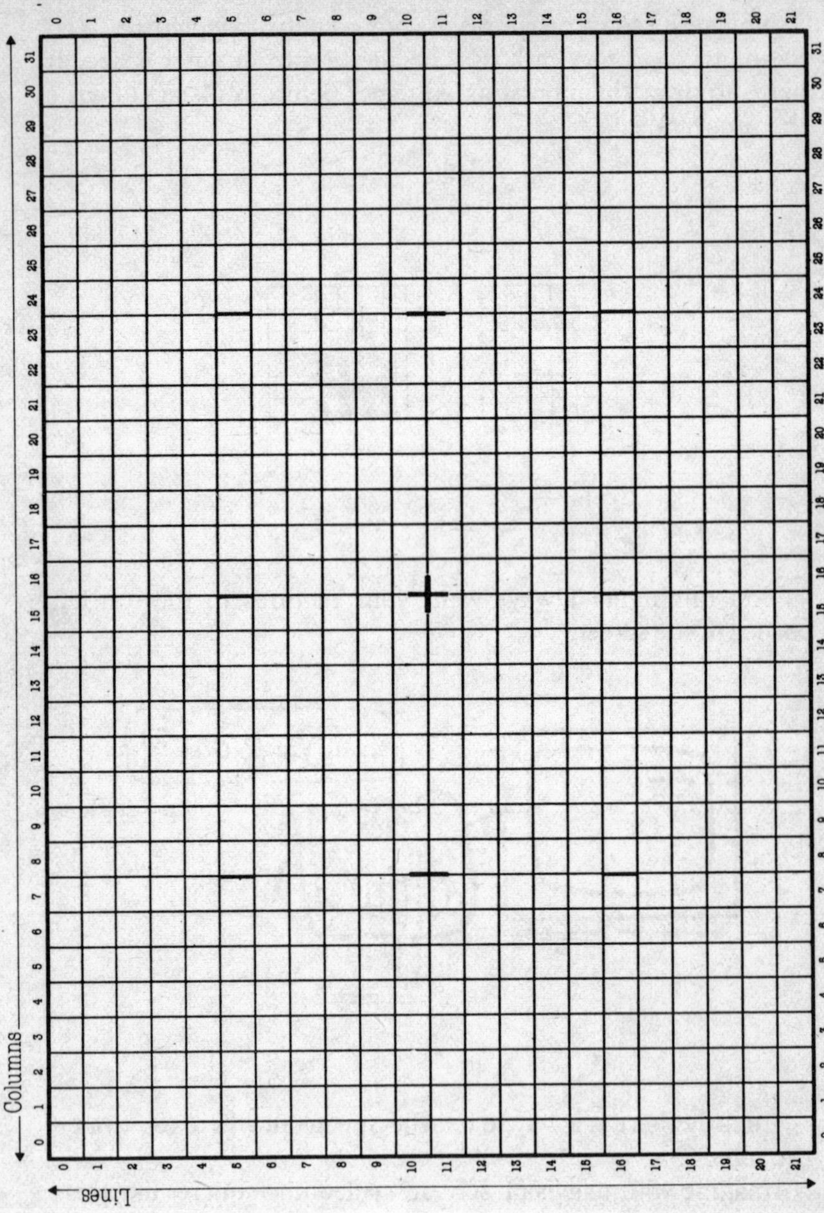
Columns
Lines

There are 22 lines, which are numbered from Ø (top line) to 21 (bottom line).

0
1
2
3
4
5
6
7
8 Spectrum
9
10
11
12
13
14
15
16
17
18
19
20
21

There are 32 columns, which are numbered from Ø (on the left) to 31 (on the right)

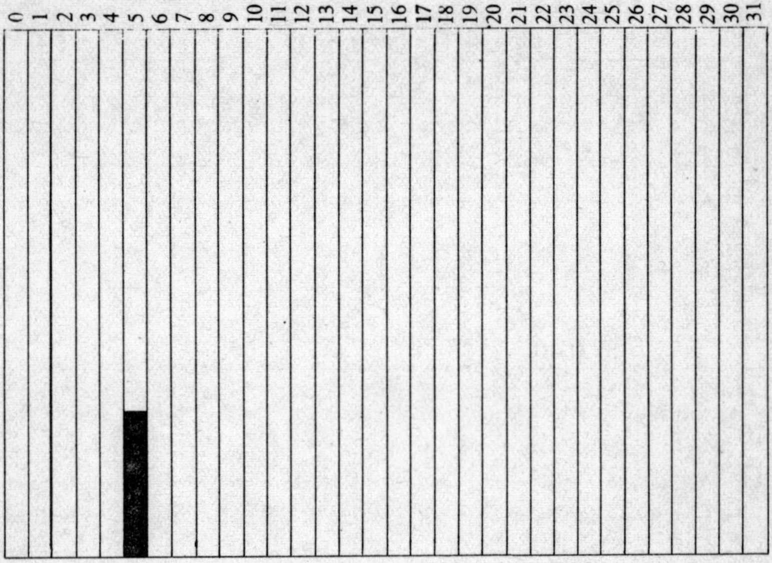

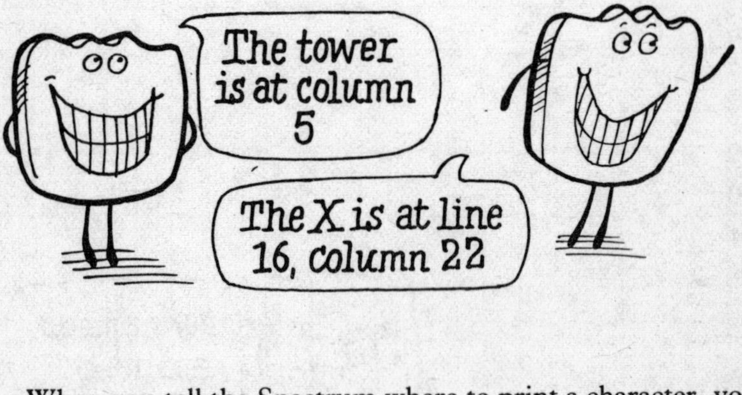

When you tell the Spectrum where to print a character, you must first give it the line number, then the column number.

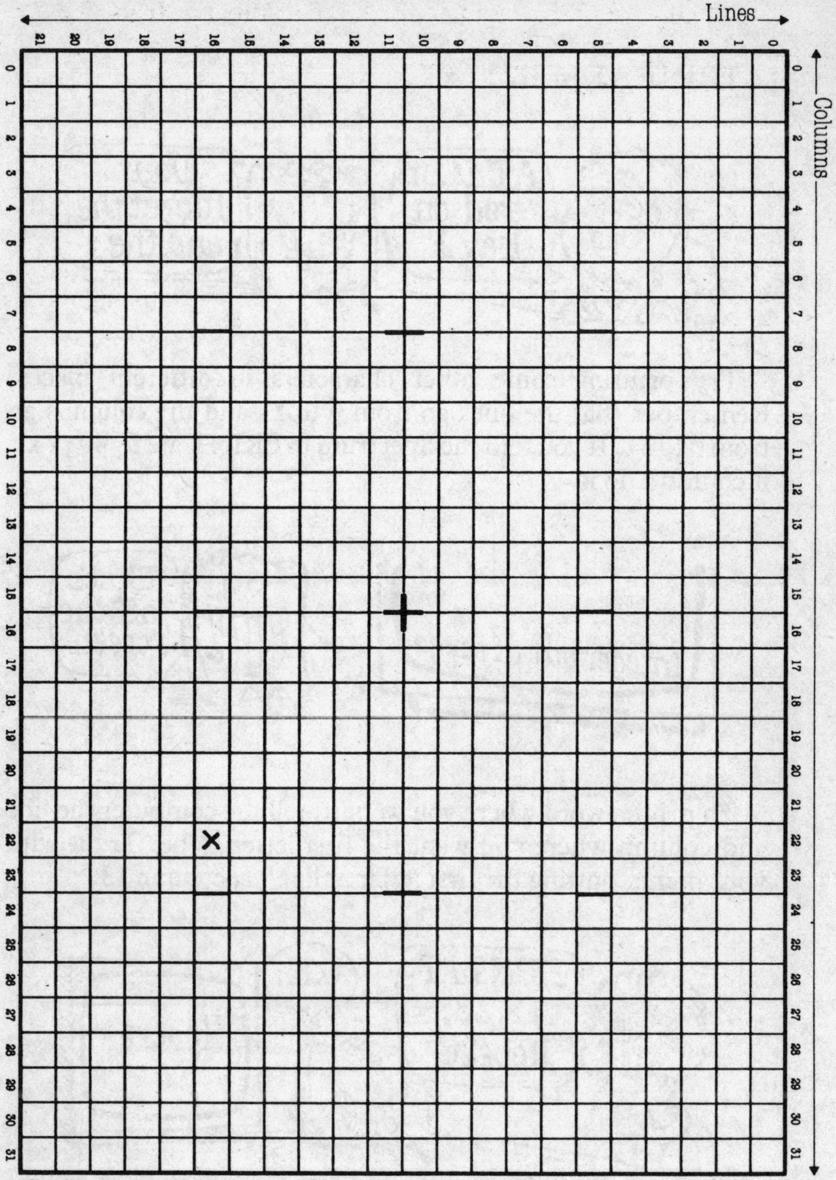
Lines
Columns

Type in

PRINT AT 16 , 22 ; " x "

Try printing some other characters in different places. Remember that the lines go from Ø to 21 and the columns go from Ø to 31. If you told the Spectrum to PRINT at 3Ø , 4Ø ; " x " it couldn't do it.

To print a word where you want it, tell the computer the line and column where you want the first letter to be. Try it with your name, putting the first letter at line 11, column 13.

Now we'll print the car at the bottom of the screen. The car is made up of two strings: "" and " O O ". We'll have the wheels on the bottom line, line 21, and the body on line 2Ø. Let's begin them both in column 6. Here is the program:

```
1Ø PRINT AT 20, 6; "
```

```
"
2Ø PRINT AT 21, 6; "O  O"
```

The next program makes it easy to design a picture which takes up as much of the screen as you want.

```
1Ø INPUT "Line ?" ; line
2Ø INPUT "Column ?" ; column
3Ø INPUT "String ?" ; s $
4Ø PRINT AT line, column; s $
5Ø GO TO 1Ø
```

RUN the program. If you want to change any part of your picture, you can print something else over the top, or just print a space there instead.

How do you stop the program when the picture is finished?

If you stop the program and then decide you want to add to the picture, just press CONT. It is short for CONTINUE, and you'll find it on key C. The program will then continue from where you stopped it.

CHAPTER 21

Colours

The Spectrum has eight colours. They are written above the number keys.

First we'll change the colour of the border round the T.V. screen. You will see the word BORDER on key B. Tell the Spectrum BORDER Ø

You can change the border in a program. This one uses a FOR . . . NEXT loop to show you the eight border colours.

```
1Ø FOR b = Ø TO 7
2Ø BORDER b
3Ø PAUSE 5Ø
4Ø NEXT b
```

You need the PAUSE 5Ø in line 3Ø, or the Spectrum will change the border colours so quickly you won't see.

The rectangle inside the border is called the PAPER. You write on it in INK.

You will find PAPER and INK below the bottom row of keys, in red letters.

To use them you will need the E cursor, and one of the SHIFT keys. Get the E cursor by pressing CAPS SHIFT and SYMBOL SHIFT. Now hold your finger on one of the SHIFT keys and press PAPER. Take your finger off SHIFT and press a number between Ø and 7. Press ENTER. Press ENTER again and the paper colour of your program listing will change.

Using the E cursor and SHIFT press INK and then a number. Press ENTER twice and your program will be written in a different coloured ink.

Here is a program which will show you what the different border, paper, and ink colours look like together:

```
10 LET b = INT (RND * 8)
20 LET p = INT (RND * 8)
30 LET i = INT (RND * 8)
40 BORDER b : PAPER p : INK i
50 PRINT "Spectrum";
60 GO TO 10
```

Do you remember in Chapter 18 we added 1 to the number the Spectrum chose, so that we never got the number Ø? We have not added one this time. We want the number Ø to come up sometimes, as black is Ø.

INT (RND * 8) gives a number from Ø to 7.

Each time it goes round the loop the Spectrum will choose the three colours at random. Why are there some places where it doesn't seem to have printed its name?

For you to do
Write a program to draw a blue flying saucer in the yellow sky above a red planet.

Start with

5 PAPER 6 : CLS

In the next line, set the INK colour to red, and print the surface of your planet at the bottom of the screen.
Then set the INK colour to blue for your saucer.

CHAPTER 22

Moving Shapes

The flying saucer from the last chapter is going to land on the planet. It will start at the top of the screen (line Ø) and stop at line 2Ø, just above the surface of the planet. We will use a loop variable called L to count the lines as it goes down.

Here is the program:

```
5 PAPER 6 : CLS
1Ø INK 2 : PRINT AT 21 , Ø ; "
```

```
"
2Ø FOR L = Ø TO 2Ø
3Ø INK 1 : PRINT AT L, 15 ; "
```

```
__"
4Ø PAUSE 2Ø
5Ø IF L < 2Ø THEN PRINT AT L, 15 ;
"      "
```

```
6Ø NEXT L
```

Line 5Ø is there to blot out one flying saucer before the next one is printed on the line beneath. My saucer is 6 characters long, so I need six spaces to blot it out. If your saucer has seven characters you will need seven spaces.

Why do we need IF L < 2Ø THEN in line 5Ø?

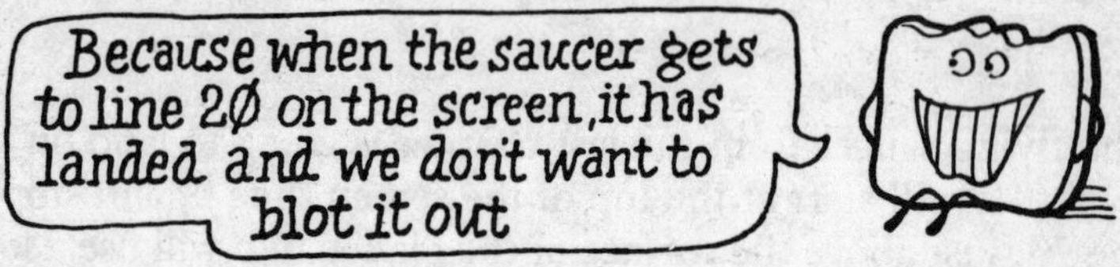

To make the saucer move faster, make the PAUSE number smaller. If you put PAUSE Ø, you will find that the saucer will stay still until you press a key. Then it will move down one line.

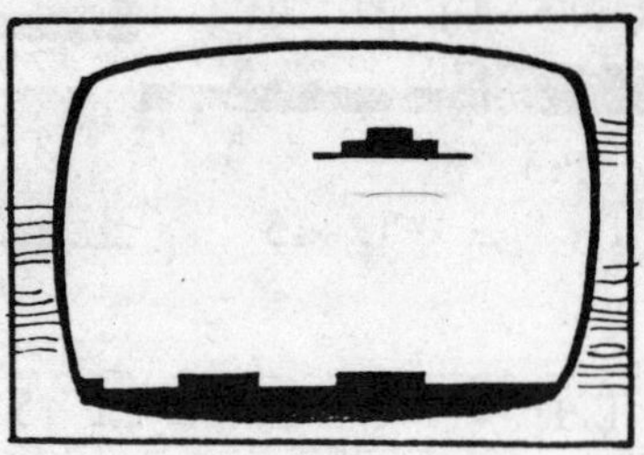

Would you like the flying saucer to take off again? Two lines of the program need to be changed:

```
2Ø FOR L = 2Ø TO Ø STEP - 1
5Ø PRINT AT L, 15 ; "       "
```

This time we start with the number 2Ø in box L so the flying saucer starts at line 2Ø on the screen. STEP − 1 tells the Spectrum how to count. At each step it must take away one from the number in L

For you to do

First set the paper colour to white and the ink colour to black so that you can read your program clearly while you are typing it in.

A white flying saucer is travelling across the sky from left to right, above a town. It is night time. The town is lit up in cyan coloured lights.

Hint: The saucer will stay on the same line of the screen, but it will move from column Ø across the screen. Use a loop variable c to count the columns.

If you make the first line of the program

```
5 PAPER Ø : CLS
```

the paper colour will change to black when you RUN the program.

CHAPTER 23

Beep, beep

To make music on your Spectrum, you tell it to BEEP. The word BEEP is in red, under key Z. Press CAPS SHIFT and SYMBOL SHIFT to get the E cursor. Put your finger on one of the shift keys and press the BEEP key.

Now you need a number to tell the Spectrum how long to beep for. The bigger the number the longer the beep. Put in number 1 and then a comma.

Now we need another number to say how high we want the sound to be. A high number gives a high sound, and a low number a low sound. Let's try 12.

BEEP 1, 12

Now press ENTER.

If you want a shorter BEEP than this, give the computer a number smaller than 1, such as .5, or .25, but don't make it too short or you won't hear it.

For those of you who can read music, this diagram will help you to write your own tunes:

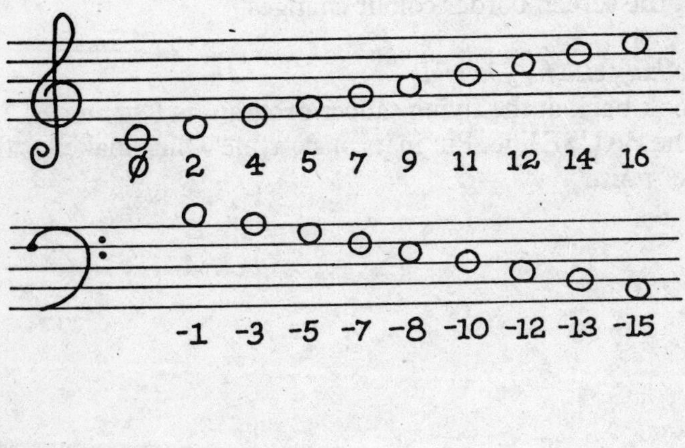

Try this program.

```
10 BEEP 1, 7 : BEEP 1, 7 : BEEP 1, 7 :
   BEEP 1, 9
20 BEEP 1, 7 : BEEP 1, 7 : BEEP 2, 2
30 BEEP 1, 4 : BEEP 1, 2 : BEEP 1, 4 :
   BEEP 1, 6
40 BEEP 2, 7 : BEEP 2, 7
```

For you to do

Write a program in which the Spectrum writes a piece of music by choosing numbers at random. Each time it plays a note, the screen border colour changes.

Something else for you to do

Look back at the flying saucer program in Chapter 22. Take out the PAUSE line. Put in its place a line which makes a "flying saucer noise".

CHAPTER 24

Inkey$

When you are playing a fast-moving game, you want the computer to act as soon as you have pressed a key, not wait until you have pressed ENTER.

Luckily, there is a word in BASIC which will help us here. It is INKEY$, which means 'the character on the key being pressed'.

Here is a short program using INKEY$:

```
1Ø PRINT INKEY$ ;
2Ø GO TO 1Ø
```

When you RUN this program, first of all the screen will go blank. Press any key. The computer will print the character on the key you are pressing. The longer you hold the key down, the more times the character will be printed. If you just tap a key very lightly, you may be able to get the Spectrum to print the character just once.

The program is a small loop. At line 1Ø, the computer looks to see if you are pressing a key. If you are, it prints the character on that key. If you are not, it moves on to line 2Ø and then back to 1Ø. The computer moves round the loop very fast indeed. Can you see why, if you hold your finger down on a key, the same character is printed again and again?

INKEY$ is not like INPUT. When the Spectrum sees INPUT, it waits for you to type something in. INKEY$ does not wait, as you will see in the next program.

```
1Ø PRINT "go" ;
2Ø IF INKEY$ = "p" THEN GO TO 4Ø
3Ø GO TO 1Ø
4Ø PRINT "stop"
```

Lines 1Ø to 3Ø are a loop. The computer goes round and round the loop, without stopping, until you press p. Pressing another letter won't do. It has to be p.

Change line 2Ø, putting in "q" instead of "p", and see what difference this makes.

For you to do:

Write a program to test how quick your reactions are.

The computer tells you to press p.

It then starts a FOR . . . NEXT loop, counting from 1 to 1000. If you press p, it jumps out of the loop and tells you how far it has counted.

CHAPTER 25

Saving your programs on cassette

When you have typed in quite a long program, you will probably want to keep it, to RUN again later. When you unplug your Spectrum the program is lost, but before you do this you can record your program onto a cassette.

You will need a cassette recorder, and a blank cassette. One of the cheaper, portable cassette recorders should work well, with a C10, C12 or C15 cassette.

Plug your cassette recorder in to the electricity (unless it runs on batteries). Put in the cassette.

With your Spectrum you have a pair of leads like this:

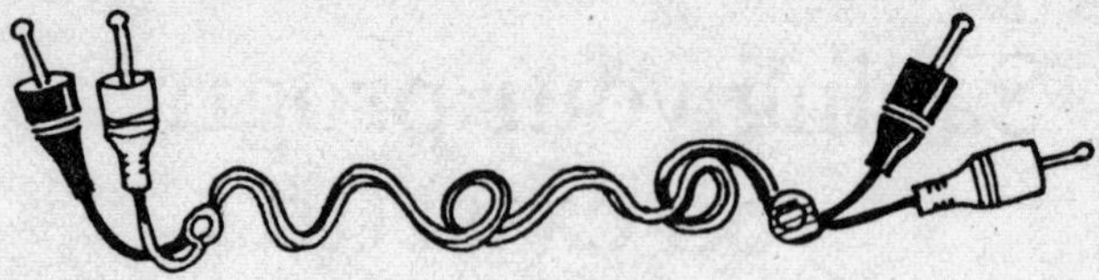

Two of the plugs are grey and two are black.

The Spectrum has two sockets at the back, side by side, called MIC and EAR.

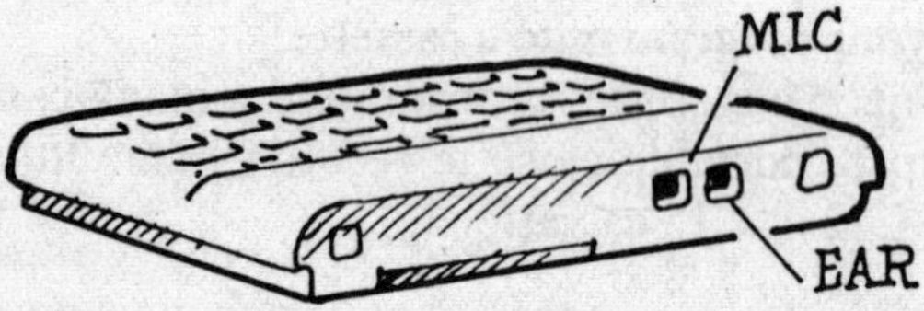

You should find your cassette recorder has, too.

Put one grey plug into the Spectrum's MIC socket, and the other grey plug into your cassette recorder's MIC socket.
Put a black plug into the Spectrum's EAR socket, but do not plug the other end in yet.

Wind the cassette back to the beginning and then move it forward just a little, so that the brown tape is showing, not the coloured plastic leader tape. Set the volume control to fairly loud (about 7 if it has 10 numbers). If there is a tone control put it to high.

Make sure the listing of your program is on the screen.

You must give your program a name. If you are saving the music program from chapter 23 you could call it "music". You can use letters or numbers for your program name. It must not be longer than ten characters.

Press the SAVE key, and type in the name of your program, with quote marks round it. Press ENTER.

You see the message:

Start tape, then press any key.

Set the cassette recorder to record, and then press any key. You will see coloured lines moving up the screen, a short break, then more coloured lines. The OK message shows that the Spectrum has finished saving the program. Stop the cassette recorder.

Now you can ask the Spectrum to check that the program really is on the cassette.

Rewind the cassette to the beginning. Take the small grey plug out of the cassette recorder's MIC socket. Put the black plug into the EAR socket.

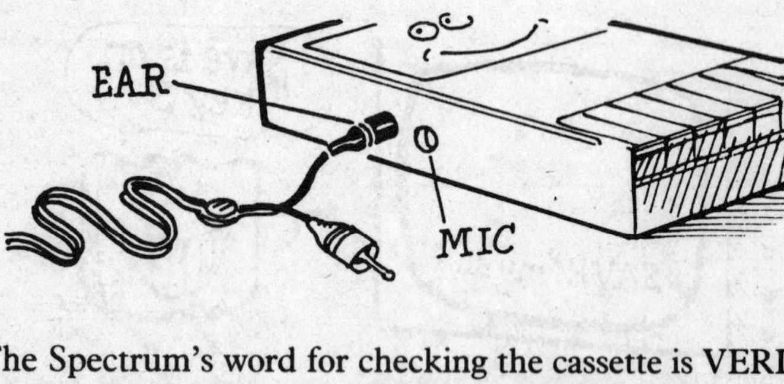

The Spectrum's word for checking the cassette is VERIFY. It is below key R. You need the E cursor and SHIFT.

Press VERIFY and type in your program name (with quote marks). Press the play button on the cassette recorder.
Press ENTER.

You should see the same coloured lines on the screen. Part of the way through, the name of your program will come up on the screen. When you see the OK message you know all is well.

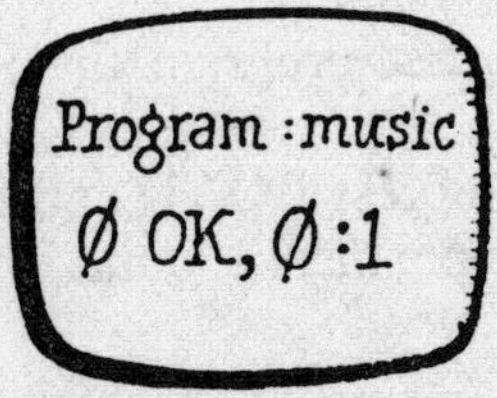

If you do not get the OK, something is wrong. Check that the leads are plugged in to the correct sockets. Turn the volume up a little on the cassette recorder. Ask the computer to VERIFY again. If this doesn't work you will have to turn back to page 88 and try saving again.

With your program safely on cassette you can turn the Spectrum off, or write another program.

When you want to put your program back into the Spectrum from the cassette, you use the word LOAD.

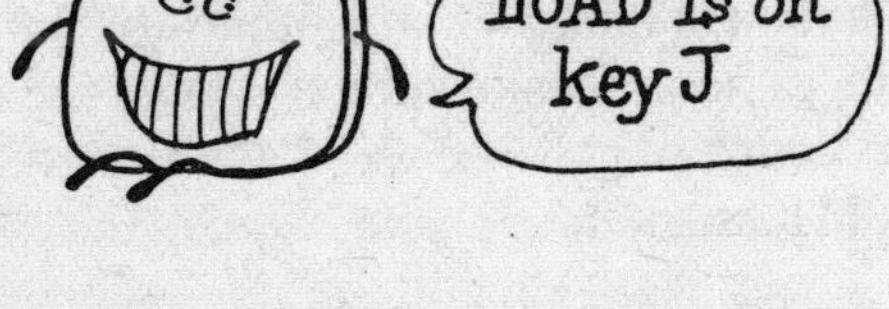

There are two ways of telling the computer to LOAD.

One way is

LOAD ""

which will load the first program the Spectrum sees on the cassette.

The other way is to press LOAD and then type the name of your program with quote marks round it.

If you have more than one program on a cassette, the second way is better, as it will find the right program.

Rewind your cassette. Make sure you have the black plug in the cassette recorder's EAR socket. Take the grey plug out of the recorder's MIC socket.

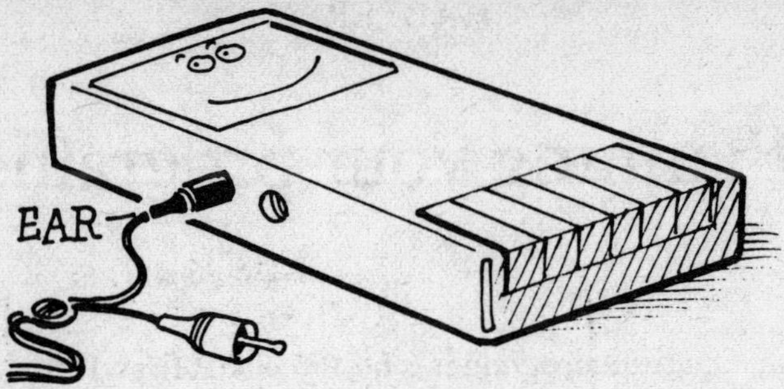

Press ENTER. You will see coloured lines across the screen. The name of your program will come up, and then the OK message.

Your program is now ready to RUN.

CHAPTER 26

Planning your programs

When you write a program it is best to plan it first. If you just sit down at the computer and start typing you will often find you get in a muddle, or leave out something important.

We are going to plan a program called "Three Mice". First of all we'll write down what we want it to do.

The computer will choose three colours. Then it will show three mice on the screen, one at a time, one of each colour. It will ask you what colours they were. You enter the numbers for the three colours. The computer checks to see if you were right. If you were right, it covers the screen with "Well done", and plays two musical notes. If you were wrong, it covers the screen with "wrong", and plays a long low note. Now we will make a list of the variables, or boxes, we will use.

We will put the mouse picture into a$.

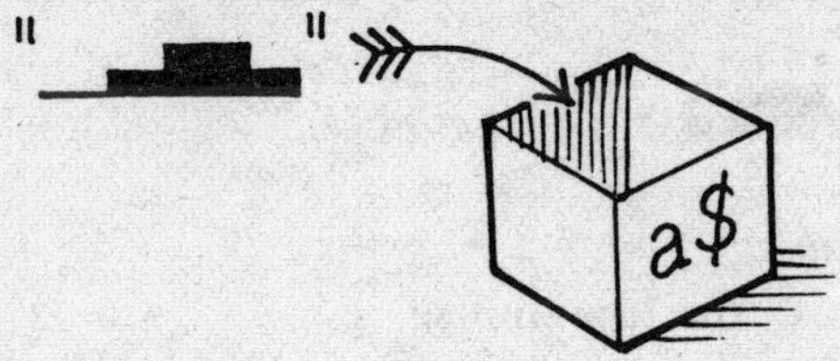

The three colours the computer chooses will go into cl, c2 and c3.

Your three guesses at the colours will go into gl, g2 and g3.

The loop for covering the screen with "WRONG" will be called a, and the one for "WELL DONE" will be b.

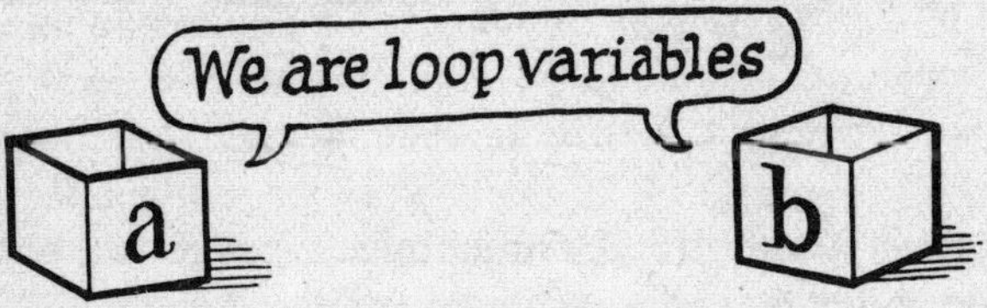

Here is the complete list:

String variable

a$  a mouse

Number variables

c1 the colour of the first mouse
c2 the colour of the second mouse
c3 the colour of the third mouse
g1 your guess at the first colour
g2 your guess at the second colour
g3 your guess at the third colour

Loop variables

a loop for printing "WRONG"
b loop for printing "WELL DONE"

When you are typing in the program, you can put in "reminder lines". The computer won't take any notice of them, but when you look back at the program later, you will remember what each part of the program does.

The Spectrum's word for reminder is REM.

Now we'll write the "Three mice" program, putting in REMinder lines.

```
10 REM Three mice
20 REM The mouse
30 LET a$ = "
```

```
"

40 REM The computer chooses three colours
50 LET c1 = INT (RND * 7)
60 LET c2 = INT (RND * 7)
70 LET c3 = INT (RND * 7)
80 REM It shows the three mice
90 INK c1 : PRINT AT 10, 14; a$
100 PAUSE 20 : CLS
110 INK c2 : PRINT AT 10, 14; a$
120 PAUSE 20 : CLS
130 INK c3 : PRINT AT 10, 14; a$
140 PAUSE 20 : CLS
```

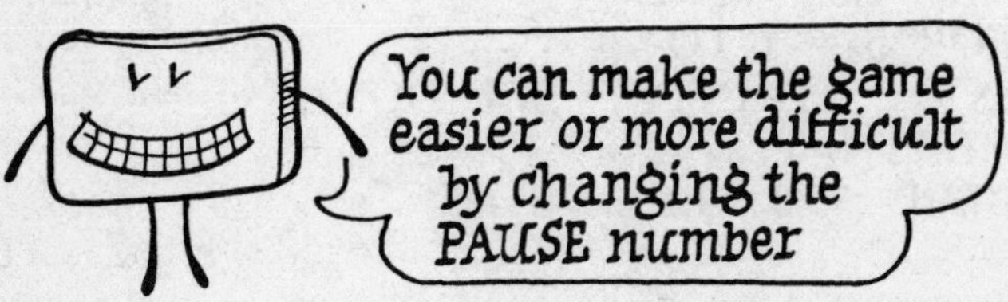


```
150 REM You guess
160 INPUT "first colour?"; g1
170 INPUT "second colour?"; g2
180 INPUT "third colour?"; g3
190 REM The computer checks your numbers
200 IF g1 = c1 AND g2 = c2 AND g3 = c3
THEN GO TO 270
```

```
210 REM  Wrong answer
220 FOR a = 1 TO 140
230 INK 1 : PRINT "WRONG";
240 NEXT a
250 BEEP 2, - 12
260 STOP
```

```
270 REM  Right answer
280 FOR b = 1 TO 70
290 INK 2 : PRINT "WELL DONE ";
300 NEXT b
310 BEEP .5, 0 : BEEP .5, 12
```

CHAPTER 27

You could do it like this

Here are some ways of answering the questions in the earlier chapters. There are many good ways of answering each question. These are just suggestions.

Chapter 6

```
1Ø PRINT "John Smith,"
2Ø PRINT "12 Old Street,"
3Ø PRINT "Romtown."
```

Did you remember to put quote marks before and after what you wanted the computer to print?

Chapter 8

```
1Ø PRINT "********************
************"
```

You need 32 stars to fill the top line of the screen.

Chapter 10

```
1Ø PRINT "What is your name?"
2Ø INPUT a$
25 PRINT
3Ø PRINT "Hello "; a$
```

or

```
10 PRINT "What is your name?"
20 INPUT a$
30 PRINT ' "Hello "; a$
```

or

```
10 PRINT "What is your name?"
20 INPUT a$
30 PRINT ,, "Hello "; a$
```

Did you find any other ways?

Chapter 11

```
10 PRINT "Where do you live?"
20 INPUT p$
30 PRINT
40 PRINT p$
50 PRINT "is a pleasant place to live."
```

Chapter 14

```
10 INPUT NUMBER 1
20 INPUT NUMBER 2
30 LET ANSWER = NUMBER 1 * NUMBER 2
40 PRINT ANSWER
```

It doesn't matter whether you use capital or small letters. The computer knows that ANSWER is the same as answer.

Chapter 16

Answer to no. 1

Suggestion for no. 2

```
10 PRINT "What is your favourite food?"
20 INPUT f$
30 CLS
40 IF f$ < > "chips" THEN PRINT "
Surely not "; f$; " ? " ' "I prefer chips." : STOP
50 PRINT "I agree. Chips are great."
```

Chapter 17

```
10 PRINT " Give me a name."
20 INPUT n$
30 IF n$ = "end" THEN STOP
40 PRINT n$
50 GO TO 10
```

Chapter 18

```
10 LET a = INT (RND * 100) +1
20 LET b = INT (RND * 100) +1
30 LET c = a + b
40 PRINT a ; " + " ; b ; " = " ;
50 INPUT d
60 PRINT d
70 IF d = c THEN PRINT "Well done."
     : STOP
80 PRINT "No. It is " ; c
```

See if you can change the program, so that you can try again if you are wrong.

Then change the program again so that you are allowed three tries only.

Look back at the guessing program. That should give you some ideas on how to do it.

Chapter 19

Program 1

```
10 FOR a = 1 to 20
20 PRINT a ; " * 16 = " ; a * 16
30 NEXT a
```

Program 2

```
10 FOR a = 1 TO 704
20 PRINT " ? " ;
30 NEXT a
```

Chapter 21

There are very many ways. Here is one suggestion:

```
 5  PAPER 6 : CLS
10  INK 2 : PRINT AT 21, 0 ; " █▄▄▄▄▄
    ▄▄▄▄█▄▄▄▄▄▄█▄▄▄▄▄▄▄"
20  INK 1 : PRINT AT 10, 15; " _▄█
    ▄_"
```

Line 10 draws the surface of the planet in red. The graphics characters are SHIFT 8 and SHIFT 3.

The flying saucer in line 20 is

Chapter 22

```
 5 PAPER 0 : CLS
10  INK 5 : PRINT AT 21, 0 ;      " █▄▄▄█▄█
▄ ▌▌▌ ▄▄ ▄▄▄ ▌▌ ▄▄ ▄ "

20  FOR c = 0 TO 26
30  INK 7 : PRINT AT 6, c; " _▄█▄_    "
40  PAUSE  10
50  PRINT  AT  6, c; "              "
60  NEXT c
```

Can you answer this question?

Chapter 23

```
1Ø  FOR m = 1 TO 16
2Ø  LET a = INT (RND * 8)
3Ø  BORDER a
4Ø  BEEP 1, a
5Ø  NEXT m
```

or

```
1Ø  LET b = INT (RND * 8)
2Ø  LET n = INT (RND * 8)
3Ø  BORDER b
4Ø  BEEP 1, n
5Ø  GO TO 1Ø
```

Chapter 24

```
10 PRINT "Press p"
20 FOR a = 1 TO 1000
30 IF INKEY$ = "p" THEN GO TO 50
40 NEXT a
50 PRINT "I counted to    "; a
```

CHAPTER 28

Games

Star Machine

Star machine is based on the "fruit machine" idea. Instead of different fruits flashing before your eyes, you have different coloured stars. When you wish to 'hold' the stars, you press key p. If you then have three of the same colour you score 10 points. Two the same colour scores 5 points. You are allowed to 'hold' the stars 25 times. See if you can break the bank with 1ØØ points.

The program is written using only the BASIC words you have met in this book, together with the words AND and OR (and I'm sure you know what they mean!) You'll see INKEY$ in action in this game.

Each section starts with a REM to let you know what is going on.

Here is a list of the variables used in the program:

Variables list

score this starts at Ø
turns this also starts at Ø

a the three colours chosen
b for the three stars
c

r$ this variable appears at line 19Ø, INPUT r$. It doesn't matter what goes into r$. The line is just there to make the computer wait till you are ready before it starts the stars rolling.

Changes you can make

Star machine is really a game of chance. The stars roll so quickly, it is really luck when you hold stars of the same colour. To make it a game of skill, put a PAUSE in after each star is printed. Try different lengths of PAUSE and see which gives the best game. (Lines 21Ø, 24Ø and 27Ø).

Other things you might like to change are the number of turns you can have (line 33Ø), the score which breaks the bank (line 175), and the sounds which you hear at various stages of the game. You might also like the number of 'rolls' you have had to be displayed on the screen.

Perhaps you could put in an extra line, so that three red stars will give you 15 points.

```
   10 REM Star Machine
   20 REM Screen Display
   30 BORDER 7: PAPER 7: INK 0: C
LS
   40 PRINT AT 6,12;""
   50 PRINT AT 7,12;""
   60 PRINT AT 8,12;""
   70 PRINT AT 9,12;""
   80 PRINT AT 10,12;""
   90 PRINT AT 11,12;""
  100 PRINT AT 12,12;""
  110 PRINT AT 13,12;""
  120 PRINT AT 14,12;""
```

```
 130 PRINT AT 17,6;"Press ENTER
to roll"
 140 PRINT AT 18,6;"Press p to h
old"
 150 REM Score and turns
 160 LET score=0: LET turns=0
 170 INK 0: PRINT AT 7,13;score
 175 IF score>99 THEN GO TO 350
 180 REM Roll
 190 INPUT r$
 195 REM Print stars and check
for hold
 200 LET a=INT (RND*6)+1
 210 INK a: PRINT AT 10,14;"*"
 220 IF INKEY$="p" THEN GO TO 30
0
 230 LET b=INT (RND*6)+1
 240 INK b: PRINT AT 10,15;"*"
 250 IF INKEY$="p" THEN GO TO 30
0
 260 LET c=INT (RND*6)+1
 270 INK c: PRINT AT 10,16;"*"
 280 IF INKEY$="p" THEN GO TO 30
0
 290 GO TO 200
 300 REM Hold
 305 LET turns=turns+1
 315 IF a=b AND b=c THEN LET sco
re=score+10: BEEP 1,0: BEEP 1,4:
 BEEP 1,7: GO TO 330
 320 IF a=b OR a=c OR b=c THEN L
ET score=score+5: BEEP 1,0: BEEP
 1,4
 330 IF turns<26 THEN GO TO 170
 340 REM time's up
 345 INK 1: PRINT AT 0,6;"Time's
 up": BEEP 4,-12: STOP
 350 REM victory
 360 INK 2: PRINT AT 0,4;"You ha
ve broken the bank": FOR l=1 TO
5: BEEP .25,12: BEEP .25,14: NEX
T l: STOP
```

Press ENTER to roll
Press p to hold

Time's up

Press ENTER to roll
Press p to hold

You have broken the bank

Press ENTER to roll
Press p to hold

Morse Mole

A mole is hidden underground in a square plot of ground 22 squares by 22 squares, and you have to find it. You may move North, South, East or West. The mole will send you messages, in morse code, to tell you which way to go. See if you can find it in ten moves or less.

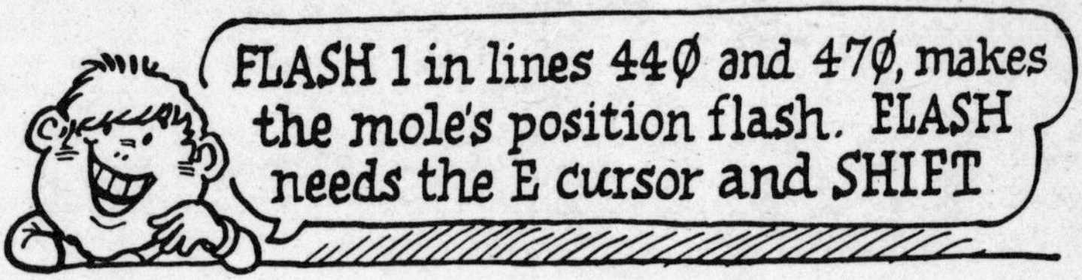

The morse code letters for the four compass points are
●   ● ● ●   – ● and ● – –

I won't tell you which is which. You can work that out from the program!

Variables list

l	the line where the mole is.
c	the column where the mole is.
ll	the line where you are.
cc	the column where you are.
s	the number of steps you wish to take.
d$	the direction you wish to move.
z	loop to change the right side of the screen to white.
m	loop for your moves.
v	loop to play the 'victory' sound.

Changes you can make

If you find the mole hunt too easy (or too difficult!) change the number of moves you can have (line 19Ø).

You always start at the bottom line of the screen. Change line

150 so that the computer chooses which line you start at.

At the moment you could start in the same place as the mole, and you wouldn't know it. Do you think, if this happens, the victory sound should play? Or would it be better for the computer to go back and choose another position for you? Put in an extra line (165) to solve this problem.

```
 10 REM morse mole
 20 REM screen
 30 BORDER 7: PAPER 0: CLS
 40 PAPER 7
 50 FOR z=0 TO 21
 60 PRINT AT z,22;"          "
 70 NEXT z
 80 INK 2: PRINT AT 1,27;"N";AT
2,27;"█"
 90 PRINT AT 3,25;"W███E"
100 PRINT AT 4,27;"█";AT 5,27;"
S"
110 REM position of mole
120 LET l=INT (RND*22)
130 LET c=INT (RND*22)
140 REM your position
150 LET ll=21
160 LET cc=INT (RND*22)
170 INK 4: PRINT AT ll,cc;"█"
180 REM your move
190 FOR m=1 TO 10
200 INPUT "Direction? (N,S,E or
W)";d$
210 INPUT "How many steps?";s
```

```
 220 REM work out your new posit
ion
 230 IF d$="N" OR d$="n" THEN LE
T ll=ll-s
 240 IF d$="S" OR d$="s" THEN LE
T ll=ll+s
 250 IF d$="E" OR d$="e" THEN LE
T cc=cc+s
 260 IF d$="W" OR d$="w" THEN LE
T cc=cc-s
 270 REM check you are still in
the black square
 280 IF ll>21 THEN LET ll=21
 290 IF ll<0 THEN LET ll=0
 300 IF cc>21 THEN LET cc=21
 310 IF cc<0 THEN LET cc=0
 320 REM see if you have found t
he mole
 330 IF ll=l AND cc=c THEN GO TO
 460
 340 REM Print your new position
 350 PRINT AT ll,cc;"█"
 360 REM Mole's response
 370 IF ll>l THEN BEEP .3,6: PAU
SE 5: BEEP .1,6: PAUSE 15
 380 IF ll<l THEN BEEP .1,6: PAU
SE 5: BEEP .1,6: PAUSE 5: BEEP .
1,6: PAUSE 15
 390 IF cc<c THEN BEEP .1,6
 400 IF cc>c THEN BEEP .1,6: PAU
SE 5: BEEP .3,6: PAUSE 5: BEEP .
3,6
 410 REM Go back for your next m
ove
 420 NEXT m
 430 REM No more moves
 440 INK 0: PRINT FLASH 1;AT l,c
;"X"
 450 BEEP 4,0: STOP
 460 REM Victory
 470 INK 2: PRINT FLASH 1;AT l,c
;"X"
 480 FOR v=1 TO 4
 490 BEEP .1,6: PAUSE 5: BEEP .1
,6: PAUSE 5: BEEP .1,6: PAUSE 15
: BEEP .3,6: PAUSE 15
 500 NEXT v
```

Mind Reader

This program shows how you can have a long conversation with your Spectrum. It is based on the "think of a number" game. Spectrumo, the great mind reader, sets out to discover the number you have thought of. I have given the computer a personality – rather arrogant, and sometimes rude.

Variables list

a$ your name.
b$ your answer to the question (yes or no).
a the number Spectrumo tells you to multiply by.
b the number Spectrumo tells you to add.
d the number Spectrumo tells you to subtract.
t loop variable to make Spectrumo's brain tick 5 times.

Changes you can make

I have not put in any colour. You could put in a line 5, to set the border, paper and ink colours, such as:

```
5 BORDER Ø: PAPER 7: INK 2: CLS.
```

Or you could change the colours at various points in the program. You might also like to put in more sound effects.

If you think Spectrumo is too rude, change his words to make him polite instead.

Another question you could put in at the end is, "Would you like me to read your mind again?" If the human player answers "yes", the computer would clear the screen and start again. A line like this will make the computer do just that:

```
65Ø IF b$ = "y" THEN RUN
```

```
  10 REM mind reader
  20 PRINT "Let me introduce mys
elf."''"I am Spectrumo, the grea
t mind  reader."
  30 PAUSE 100
  40 PRINT ''"Please introduce y
ourself to me,by typing your nam
e."
  50 INPUT a$
  60 CLS
  70 PRINT "Greetings, ";a$;"."
  75 PAUSE 100
  80 PRINT ''"Please think of a
number."''"Do NOT tell me what i
t is."
  90 PAUSE 100
 100 PRINT ''"Are you ready?"
 110 INPUT "y or n";b$
 120 IF b$="y" THEN GO TO 150
 130 IF b$="n" THEN CLS : PRINT
"Come on, ";a$;"."''"Get your br
ain cells working.": GO TO 90
 140 GO TO 110
 150 CLS
 155 LET a=(INT (RND*5)+1)*2
 160 PRINT "Now, ";a$;"."''"Mult
iply your number by ";a;"."
 170 PAUSE 100
 180 PRINT ''"Ready?"
 190 INPUT "y or n";b$
 200 IF b$="y" THEN GO TO 230
 210 IF b$="n" THEN CLS : PRINT
"You need to learn your tables,"
''a$;".": GO TO 170
 220 GO TO 190
 230 CLS
 240 PRINT "Right.  Let us move
on."
 250 PAUSE 100
 260 LET b=(INT (RND*5)+1)*2
 270 PRINT ''"Add ";b;"."
 280 PAUSE 100
 285 PRINT ''"That can't be diff
icult for you,"'a$;"."
 290 PAUSE 100
 295 PRINT ''"Have you done it?"
 300 INPUT "y or n";b$
 310 IF b$="y" THEN GO TO 340
 320 IF b$="n" THEN CLS : PRINT
"I am surprised at you, ";a$;"!"
: GO TO 290
 330 GO TO 300
 340 CLS
 350 PRINT "Good."
```

```
 360 PAUSE 100
 370 PRINT ''"Now divide by two.
"''"In other words, halve it."
 380 PAUSE 100
 390 PRINT ''"Are you ready yet,
";a$;"?"
 400 INPUT "y or n";b$
 410 IF b$="y" THEN GO TO 440
 420 IF b$="n" THEN CLS : PRINT
"Come on, ";a$;"."''"I do not li
ke to be kept          waiting.":
GO TO 380
 430 GO TO 400
 440 LET d=INT (RND*b)+1: CLS
 450 PRINT "Lastly, take away ";
d;"."
 460 PAUSE 100
 470 PRINT ''"When you have done
 this,          type in the number
 you now have."
 480 PRINT ''"I shall use my ama
zing powers   to tell you the nu
mber you firstthought of."
 490 INPUT n
 500 CLS
 510 PRINT "Please excuse the ti
cking of my brain."
 520 FOR t=1 TO 5
 530 BEEP .5,-30: BEEP .5,-32
 540 NEXT t
 550 LET fn=(((n+d)*2)-b)/a
 560 CLS : PRINT "The number you
 first thought of"''"was ";fn;".
"
 570 PAUSE 100
 580 PRINT ''"Am I right?"
 590 INPUT "y or n";b$
 600 CLS
 610 IF b$="y" THEN PRINT "You m
ust agree I am the most    marve
llous mind reader."
 620 IF b$="n" THEN PRINT "It is
 impossible for a great    mind
reader such as I to be     wrong
."''"You must have made a mistak
e in your Maths."
```

Alien

An alien is trying to land on earth. You have a gun, and must try to shoot him before he reaches the ground. To fire you press "Ø". To move left you press "5" and to move right you press "8". Your bullets look like small arrows(↑).

The only part which uses BASIC words not covered in this book is the section from line 3Ø to line 6Ø, which draws new graphics characters (the alien and the man with a gun), and stores them in the computer's memory.

Variables list

l	the line the alien is on.
c	the column the alien is in.
ll	the line where you are.
cc	the column where you are.
m	a random number chosen by the computer between Ø and 2. If it is Ø, the alien moves left. If it is 1, the alien moves right. If it is 2, the alien stays in the same column.
f	loop variable to print your bullet going up the screen.
b	loop variable to play the "alien is dead" sound.
g a	variables used in defining the two new graphics characters.

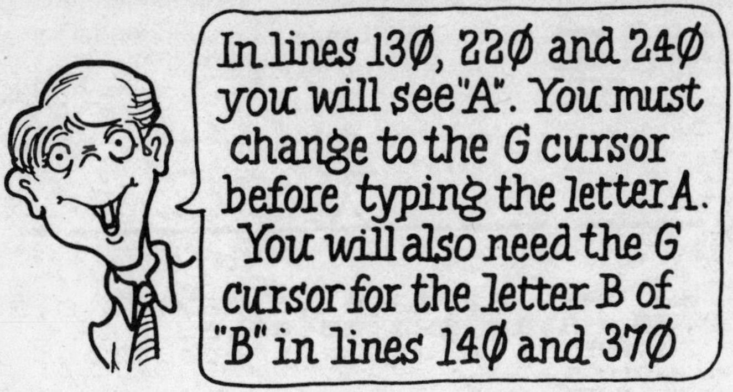

You will notice that the last line of the program changes the border and the paper colours back to white, and the ink to black. This is so that when you LIST the program, ready to make changes, it will be easy to read.

Changes you can make

Instead of just one alien, let's have a steady stream of them, say 1Ø. Put in a FOR . . . NEXT loop for this. Start the loop at line 65. The end of the loop will be at line 4ØØ, so move the present line 4ØØ to line 41Ø.

Make the computer count how many aliens you manage to shoot. You will need a number variable called score. Set it to Ø before the game starts (say at line 65). Choose whereabouts on the screen you want the score to be printed, and put in a line 165 to tell the computer to do this. When you destroy an alien the number in score must go up by one. Put this instruction in line 31Ø, just before GO TO 4ØØ.

If you want to make the game easier, or more difficult, change the length of the BEEP in line 22Ø.

```
10 REM alien
20 REM define graphics
30 FOR g=0 TO 15
40 READ a: POKE USR "a"+g,a
50 NEXT g
```

```
  60 DATA 62,42,62,8,127,73,8,54
,2,58,56,18,124,16,40,68
  70 REM fix alien's position, a
nd yours
  80 LET l=0: LET c=INT (RND*20)
+6
  90 LET ll=20: LET cc=16
 100 REM print screen
 110 BORDER 0: PAPER 0: CLS
 120 PRINT INK 4;AT 21,6;"████████
██████████████████"
 130 PRINT INK 5;AT l,c;"A"
 140 PRINT INK 6;AT ll,cc;"B"
 150 REM start game
 160 REM alien moves
 170 LET m=INT (RND*3)
 180 PRINT AT l,c;" "
 190 IF m=0 AND c>6 THEN LET c=c
-1
 200 IF m=1 AND c<25 THEN LET c=
c+1
 210 IF l<20 THEN LET l=l+1
 220 PRINT INK 5;AT l,c;"A": BEE
P .01,12
 230 REM check if alien has land
ed
 240 IF l=20 THEN PRINT INK 5; F
LASH 1;AT l,c;"A": BEEP 1,-5: BE
EP .5,-7: BEEP 1,-5: BEEP .5,-7:
 GO TO 400
 250 REM you fire
 260 IF INKEY$<>"0" THEN GO TO 3
20
 270 FOR f=19 TO 0 STEP -1
 280 PRINT INK 7;AT f,cc;"+"
 290 PRINT AT f,cc;" "
 300 NEXT f
 310 IF c=cc THEN FOR b=1 TO 4:
BEEP .5,-1: BEEP .5,0: NEXT b: G
O TO 400
 330 REM you move
 340 PRINT AT ll,cc;" "
```

```
 350 IF INKEY$="5" AND cc>6 THEN
 LET cc=cc-1
 360 IF INKEY$="8" AND cc<25 THE
N LET cc=cc+1
 370 PRINT INK 6;AT ll,cc;"B"
 380 GO TO 160
 400 BORDER 7: PAPER 7: INK 0: S
TOP
```

"Elephant" and "Catherine Wheels" are slightly longer programs, and include several new BASIC words which I have not explained in this book. I have included them to show you some of the things you can do when you have learnt more about programming your Spectrum.

Elephant

Elephant is a game of chance, but you have to keep your wits about you. The object is to "build" your elephant before your opponent does.

You must throw a six for its body, a five for the tail, four for the legs, three for the head, two for the trunk and one for the eye. After each throw of the die, the Spectrum will ask you whether you can use this number to add to your elephant.

There are four things to remember:

1. You must give the elephant a body first of all.
2. You may not give it an eye or a trunk until it has a head.
3. Once you have used a number, you cannot use the same number again. For example, if your elephant already has a tail, you cannot use the number five.
4. The computer will not let you cheat! Try it, and see what happens.

Three new BASIC words are used in this program – DIM, GO SUB, and RETURN. They are all keywords, so when you need them, just press the keys on which they are written.

```
   10 REM elephant
   20 REM variables
   30 DIM p$(2,12): DIM r(2,6): D
IM c(2)
   40 LET c(1)=0: LET c(2)=15
   42 REM enter names
   45 INK 0: PRINT AT 0,12;"Eleph
ant"
   50 LET x=7: FOR a=1600 TO 1100
 STEP -100: GO SUB a: NEXT a
   60 FOR a=1 TO 2
   70 INPUT ("Player ";a)'"Enter
your first name, please."'p$(a)
   80 NEXT a
   90 GO TO 2000
  100 REM print dice
  110 GO SUB 230: RETURN
  120 GO SUB 200: GO SUB 260: RET
URN
  130 GO SUB 200: GO SUB 230: GO
SUB 260: RETURN
  140 GO SUB 200: GO SUB 210: GO
SUB 250: GO SUB 260: RETURN
  150 GO SUB 200: GO SUB 210: GO
SUB 230: GO SUB 250: GO SUB 260:
 RETURN
  160 GO SUB 200: GO SUB 210: GO
SUB 220: GO SUB 240: GO SUB 250:
 GO SUB 260: RETURN
  200 PRINT AT 5,x;a$: RETURN
  210 PRINT AT 5,x+2;a$: RETURN
  220 PRINT AT 6,x;a$: RETURN
  230 PRINT AT 6,x+1;a$: RETURN
  240 PRINT AT 6,x+2;a$: RETURN
  250 PRINT AT 7,x;a$: RETURN
  260 PRINT AT 7,x+2;a$: RETURN
  300 REM remove elephant
  310 FOR a=10 TO 15
  320 PRINT AT a,c(p)+3;"        
    ": BEEP 1,-5
  330 NEXT a
  340 FOR a=1 TO 6
  350 LET r(p,a)=0
  360 NEXT a
  370 RETURN
 1100 REM eye
 1110 PRINT AT 11,4+x;"▟"
 1120 RETURN
 1200 REM trunk
 1210 PRINT AT 13,2+x;"▐";AT 14,2
+x;"▌";AT 15,1+x;"▐"
 1220 RETURN
 1300 REM head
 1310 FOR z=10 TO 12: PRINT AT z,
3+x;"▓▓▓": NEXT z
```

```
1320 RETURN
1400 REM legs
1410 FOR z=14 TO 15: PRINT AT z,
5+x;"██    ██": NEXT z
1420 RETURN
1500 REM tail
1510 PRINT AT 10,13+x;"▚";AT 11,
14+x;"▚"
1520 RETURN
1600 REM body
1610 FOR z=10 TO 13: PRINT AT z,
5+x;"██████": NEXT z
1620 RETURN
2000 REM screen
2005 CLS
2010 INK 0: PRINT AT 0,12;"Eleph
ant"
2020 FOR b=1 TO 2
2030 PRINT INK b;AT 3,5+c(b);p$(
b)
2040 NEXT b
2050 PRINT AT 18,2;"6 body     5
tail    4 legs";AT 19,2;"3 head
    2 trunk    1 eye"
2060 REM start game
2070 FOR p=1 TO 2: INK p
2080 INPUT INK p;(p$(p))'"press
ENTER to roll the die.";d$
2085 LET x=7+c(p)
2090 FOR s=5 TO 7: PRINT AT s,x;
"     ": NEXT s
2095 LET d=INT (RND*6)+1
2100 FOR n=1 TO 6: BEEP .1,4: BE
EP .1,3: NEXT n
2105 LET a$=" ▪"
2110 GO SUB d*10+100
2115 LET c$="y": INPUT INK p;(p$
(p))'"can you use this (y or n)?
";b$
2118 IF b$<>"y" AND b$<>"n" THEN
 GO TO 2115
2120 IF r(p,d)=1 THEN LET c$="n"
2125 IF r(p,6)=0 AND d<6 THEN LE
T c$="n"
2130 IF r(p,3)=0 AND d<3 THEN LE
T c$="n"
2132 IF b$="y" AND c$="y" THEN L
ET x=c(p): GO SUB d*100+1000: LE
T r(p,d)=1
2135 IF b$="y" AND c$="n" THEN G
O SUB 300
2140 IF r(p,2)=1 AND r(p,1)=1 TH
EN GO TO 2170
2150 NEXT p
2160 GO TO 2070
```

```
2170 REM a winner
2180 LET x=c(p)
2190 FOR w=1 TO 10
2200 PRINT AT 10,13+x;" ";AT 11,
14+x;" "
2210 PRINT AT 10,13+x;"▀▀▀"
2220 PRINT AT 10,13+x;"   "
2230 PRINT AT 9,13+x;"▗▘";AT 8,14
+x;"▗▘"
2235 IF w=9 THEN GO TO 2270
2240 PRINT AT 9,13+x;" ";AT 8,14
+x;" "
2250 GO SUB 1500
2255 BEEP .1,w
2260 NEXT w
2270 PRINT FLASH 1;AT 2,5+c(p);"
Winner"
2280 INPUT "Another game? (y or
n) ";z$
2290 IF z$="y" THEN RUN
2300 IF z$="n" THEN INK 0: STOP
2310 GO TO 2280
```

Catherine Wheels

This is a word guessing game. The computer chooses a word, and shows you how many letters it has by printing a row of stars. You have to discover what the word is. You may guess the whole word, or may guess one letter at a time.

Each time you guess wrong, the man with the bucket of water moves closer to your three Catherine wheels. If you make ten wrong guesses he will pour his water over your fireworks. If, on the other hand, you manage to discover the word, your Catherine wheels will burst into life.

If you have difficulty guessing the word the computer will offer you help.

You will find the ten words, with a clue for each one, at lines 81ØØ – 9ØØØ in the program. If you want to change the words, just alter these lines, putting in, on each line, first the word, then the clue for it.

When you are typing in the program, in line 61Ø, you must change the cursor to G before typing A, B C D, and E F G. Also, in line 12Ø5, you will need the G cursor for H and I.

Of the ten new BASIC words in this program, PLOT and DRAW are keywords. RESTORE, LEN, CHR$, CODE, PI, SIN and COS need the E cursor, and BRIGHT and CIRCLE need the E cursor with SHIFT.

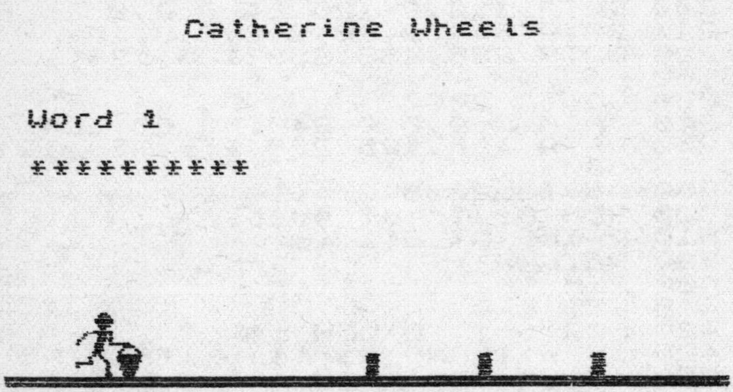

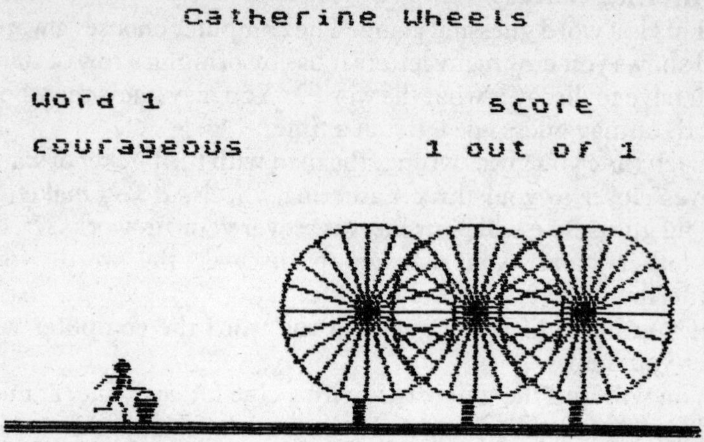


```
  10 REM Catherine Wheels
  20 BORDER 6: PAPER 7: INK 0: C
LS
 100 RESTORE 160
 110 FOR g=0 TO 71
 120 READ d
 130 POKE USR "a"+g,d
 150 NEXT g
 160 DATA 0,0,48,120,252,252,120
,48
 170 DATA 7,8,16,32,64,0,0,1
 180 DATA 252,116,116,116,231,22
4,224,192
 190 DATA 0,0,0,0,240,60,66,129
 200 DATA 1,2,2,126,64,0,0,0
 210 DATA 64,32,16,8,8,8,8,12
 220 DATA 255,255,255,126,126,12
6,60,60
 230 GO TO 2000
 240 DATA 0,0,0,0,240,60,60,126
 250 DATA 126,126,255,255,255,12
9,66,60
 260 GO TO 2000
 300 REM State of guess
 310 PRINT AT 6,1;l$
 320 RETURN
 400 REM Check letter
 410 LET k=0
 420 FOR b=1 TO LEN w$
 425 IF b>1 AND g$=l$(b) THEN RE
TURN
```

```
 430 IF g$=w$(b) THEN LET l$(b)=
g$: BEEP .1,12: GO SUB 300: LET
k=1
 440 NEXT b
 450 IF k=0 THEN LET p=p+1: GO S
UB 600
 460 RETURN
 500 REM Check word
 510 IF g$<>w$ THEN LET p=p+1: G
O SUB 600: RETURN
 520 BEEP .1,12: LET l$=w$: RETU
RN
 600 REM Draw man
 610 PRINT AT 16,p+2;"  A";AT 17
,p+2;" BCD";AT 18,p+2;" EFG"
 620 IF p>0 THEN BEEP .5,-12
 630 RETURN
 700 REM Lower case
 710 FOR l=1 TO LEN g$
 720 IF CODE g$(l)>64 AND CODE g
$(l)<91 THEN LET g$(l)=CHR$ (COD
E g$(l)+32)
 730 NEXT l
 740 RETURN
 800 REM Score
 810 PRINT AT 4,22;"score";AT 6,
19;score;" out of ";a
 820 RETURN
 900 REM Clue
 905 IF clue=1 THEN RETURN
 910 INPUT BRIGHT 1;"Shall I giv
e you a clue?"'"(y or n) ";z$
 920 IF z$="n" OR z$="N" THEN RE
TURN
 930 IF z$="y" OR z$="Y" THEN PR
INT AT 10,1;"clue";AT 12,1;m$: R
ETURN
 940 GO TO 910
1000 REM First letter
1010 INPUT BRIGHT 1;"Shall I tel
l you the first"'"letter? (y or
n) ";z$
1020 IF z$="n" OR z$="N" THEN RE
TURN
1030 IF z$="y" OR z$="Y" THEN LE
T l$(1)=w$(1): GO SUB 300: RETUR
N
1040 GO TO 1010
1100 REM Catherine Wheels
1110 FOR x=132 TO 212 STEP 40
1120 INK INT (RND*6)+1
1130 CIRCLE x,64,32
1140 FOR z=0 TO 1 STEP .05
1150 PLOT x,64: LET aa=2*PI*z
```

```
1160 DRAW 32*SIN aa,32*COS aa
1170 NEXT z: NEXT x: INK 0
1180 RESTORE 7000: FOR d=1 TO 6:
 READ du,pi
1185 BEEP du,pi: NEXT d
1190 LET score=score+1: GO SUB 8
00: RETURN
1200 REM Wet Catherine wheels
1205 PRINT AT 17,p+5;"H";AT 18,p
+5;"I"
1210 FOR c=16 TO 26 STEP 5
1220 PRINT INK 3;AT 18,c;"▀"
1230 FOR w=1 TO 5: BEEP .01,12:
NEXT w
1240 NEXT c
1250 PRINT AT 6,1;w$
1260 RETURN
1300 REM Choose word
1310 LET r=INT (RND*10)+1
1320 IF w(r)=1 THEN GO TO 1310
1330 LET w(r)=1
1340 RESTORE 8000+100*r
1350 READ w$,m$
1360 DIM l$(LEN w$)
1370 FOR s=1 TO LEN l$
1380 LET l$(s)="*": NEXT s
1390 RETURN
2000 REM Start game
2005 LET score=0: DIM w(10)
2010 FOR a=1 TO 10: CLS
2020 LET p=0: LET clue=0: LET le
t=0
2030 PRINT AT 0,8;"Catherine Whe
els"
2040 PRINT INK 4;AT 19,0;"██████
████████████████████████████████"
2050 PRINT INK 3;AT 18,16;"█
█    █"
2060 GO SUB 600
2070 GO SUB 1300
2080 PRINT AT 4,1;"Word ";a
2100 GO SUB 300
2110 IF l$=w$ THEN GO SUB 1100:
GO TO 2220
2120 IF p=4 THEN GO SUB 900: LET
 clue=1
2130 IF p=7 AND l$(1)="*" AND le
t=0 THEN GO SUB 1000: LET let=1:
 GO TO 2110
2140 INPUT "Enter your guess,"'
INK 2;"the whole word "; INK 0;"
or just"' INK 2;"one letter.";g$
2150 IF g$="" THEN GO TO 2140
2160 GO SUB 700
```

```
2170 IF LEN g$=1 THEN GO SUB 400
2180 IF LEN g$>1 THEN GO SUB 500
2190 IF p<10 THEN GO TO 2100
2200 GO SUB 1200
2210 GO SUB 800
2220 IF a<10 THEN INPUT "Press E
NTER for the next word.  ";z$
2240 NEXT a
2250 INPUT "Press ENTER to play
again. ";z$
2280 RUN
7000 REM Tune
7010 DATA 1.5,7,.5,7,1.5,12,.5,1
2
7020 DATA 1.5,14,.25,16,.25,17,1
,16
8100 DATA "courageous","brave"
8200 DATA "audience","people wat
ching a play"
8300 DATA "envelope","something
to put a letter in"
8400 DATA "nourish","feed"
8500 DATA "congregation","people
 in church"
8600 DATA "breadth","width"
8700 DATA "cautious","very caref
ul"
8800 DATA "immense","huge"
8900 DATA "interrupt","break or
but in"
9000 DATA "disease","illness"
```

Index

AT 72
BEEP 82
BORDER 75
BREAK 53
Capital letters 26
Characters 28
CLS 48
DELETE 20
E cursor 55
EDIT 48
ENTER 19
FOR 61
G cursor 65
GO TO 51
Graphics 65
IF 48
INK 76
INKEY$ 85
INPUT 35
INT 57
K cursor 29
Keywords 29
L cursor 29
LET 38
LIST 47
LOAD 91
Loop variables 61
NEW 26
NEXT 61
Number variables 43
OK message 19
PAPER 76
PAUSE 63
PRINT 17
Program cursor 45
REM 96
RND 55
RUN 24
SAVE 89
Scroll 56
STEP 80
STOP 49
Strings 28
String variables 37
THEN 48
TO 61
VERIFY 90
" 18
; 31
, 31
' 32
− 40
+ 40
* 40
/ 40
← 46
↓ 47
↑ 47
→ 46
< > 48
: 49
< 59